Olwen Hawkes

Problem of the Week 6

Written by John Spooner
Edited by Sheila Ebbutt and Mike Askew

RIGBY

Rigby
Halley Court, Jordan Hill, Oxford, OX2 8EJ
a division of Reed Educational and Professional Publishing Ltd

Rigby is a registered trademark of Reed Educational and Professional Publishing Ltd

OXFORD MELBOURNE AUCKLAND
JOHANNESBURG BLANTYRE GABORONE
IBADAN PORTSMOUTH (NH) CHICAGO

Written by John Spooner
Edited by Sheila Ebbutt and Mike Askew

First published 2000

05 04 03 02 01 00
10 9 8 7 6 5 4 3 2 1

ISBN 0 435 21791 7

Typeset by DP Press Limited, Sevenoaks, Kent
Illustrated by George Hollingworth and Philip Orchard
Printed and bound by Ashford Colour Press, Gosport, Hants

Contents

Introduction

Problem of the Week is an additional **Numeracy Focus** resource providing more extended investigative activities. Presented as interesting puzzles and problems, they have been designed to stimulate children's mathematical imaginations.

There is one problem for every **Numeracy Focus** teaching unit. The activities can be used for both homework and class work, and are structured for ongoing use over the course of a week.

Each problem provides an investigative activity appropriate to the level of work being covered by the *Teaching and Learning File* that week.

The problems have the same format: the problem is introduced to the whole class, then children develop and solve it independently, then discuss their findings as a whole class.

Using and applying mathematics

The teaching approach taken in **Numeracy Focus** is to ensure that children use and apply the mathematics they learn in the dedicated daily maths lessons. There is scope, however, for children to work on larger-scale problems than a 45–60 minute lesson allows. *Problem of the Week* gives children the opportunity to engage in such larger-scale problems. Once they are introduced to the problem and understand it, they work independently on ways of solving it. Children are often given the opportunity to develop their own variations of the problems.

The problems have been written to ensure a balance between pure mathematical problems and problems that are set in a 'realistic' context. For example, Problem 4 is about fractions and decimals, but it is presented as a code breaking puzzle. Problem 5 is a practical problem involved with deciding on quantities of ingredients for a recipe. The activities present problems in an imaginative context designed to interest the children.

Organization of *Problem of the Week*

Each problem is presented on a double-page spread. On the left-hand side is the teacher's page, containing instructions on how you introduce and manage the problem. On the right-hand side is a photocopiable children's page; this can be used in a number of ways, depending on the specific problem being tackled.

The teacher's and children's pages – in detail

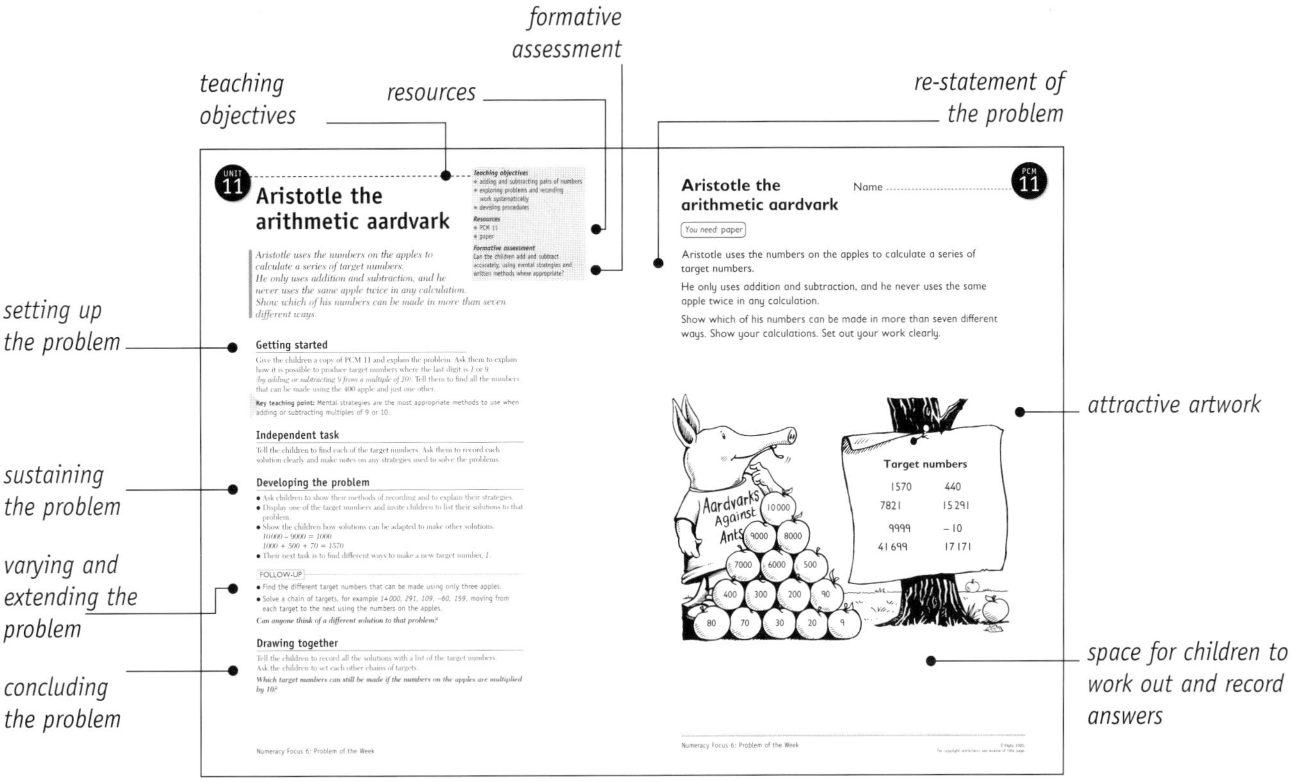

The teacher's page

Teaching objectives

There are three for each problem, one giving the mathematical content, and the other two emphasizing using and applying mathematics.

Resources

These are normally minimal because children are expected to do some of the work at home, and they may not have access to extra equipment. When work on the problem takes place in the classroom, standard classroom equipment is indicated.

Where equipment is suggested, you may need to offer alternatives. For example, some activities require the children to have counters. You could substitute real or plastic coins or cubes, depending on the type of activity.

Formative assessment

A question is given to help you assess a particular aspect of children's mathematical performance as they investigate the problem.

Getting started – Setting up the problem

All the problems need to be introduced to the children. You will need to allocate 10–15 minutes to explain the problem to the children and to discuss with them how to start work on it.

The teacher's page gives a starting activity for the children to do, such as a simpler, related activity, or a different example. This initial activity can be organized as class discussion, paired work or individual thinking. Suggestions are also made for giving children ideas about how to start work on the problem. You need to interest the children in the problem, and make sure that they have strategies for working on it on their own.

Independent task – Homework or in class

When you are setting up the problem, make sure you do not give solutions or best methods to the children. Rather, you should aim to set the children off in the right direction and then let them solve the problem in their own way.
You need to be absolutely clear about what children should tackle independently, in what way, and how much they should do. At the same time, be careful not to overload them with too much information. One way in which the independent element has been structured is for children to do an activity on their own in preparation for working on something in the classroom. For example, they might collect data in a tally chart and then use this later in class. With these problems, you should specify what the children record on their own, if anything, and how, and make it clear what they need to bring back for discussion and continuation of the investigation.

Developing the problem – Sustaining the problem

This part of the problem is for discussing the children's progress thus far. The discussion should centre on the work the children have already done. You will need to discuss with the children the different methods they are using, and examine interim solutions they have come to.

On the teacher's page there are some questions to prompt further thinking by the children, and to encourage them to reflect on what they've done. There are also hints about what to look out for, and help for those who might be stuck.

Follow-up – Varying and extending the problem

These are ideas for children who have finished the initial problem.

Drawing together – Concluding the problem

It is important to draw the whole problem together and reach a conclusion. This gives an opportunity for discussing the final results as well as explaining and justifying different methods. This also provides the opportunity for children to present their work. You could make a final presentation of the work in the classroom, such as pinning the work on a wall, making a more formal display, or making a class book. You may choose not to have any formal recording of the problem, preferring simply to discuss the children's findings and methods. Or, you could do a presentation for assembly, if appropriate.

The photocopiable page

The photocopiable page mainly serves to remind children of the problem they are trying to solve. It can also offer useful information, a way of recording children's findings, a stimulus to further ideas, or a game to play. For some problems it may be sufficient to pin up one copy in the classroom. With other problems it would be useful for children to take the page home.

Using *Problem of the Week*

As homework

Homework should be an effective and enjoyable way of developing children's numeracy skills. **Numeracy Focus** provides three forms of homework, all of which complement each other. The *Homework* book provides short puzzles, games and problems. The *Teaching and Learning File* gives one open-ended, short activity relevant to the work in that teaching unit. The *Problem of the Week* is intended to provide an interesting challenge for children to take home at the weekend, or one night during the week.

As class work

The *Problem of the Week* can also be used to provide activities in the classroom. The children can work on the problem during the main teaching activity component of the two flexible daily maths lessons in the week.

Where *Problem of the Week* fits into Numeracy Focus planning

Problem of the Week reflects the content of **Numeracy Focus**. The problems allow children to use and apply the skills they have been learning. This gives you the flexibility to introduce *Problem of the Week* when it suits you. For example, you could use *Problem of the Week* as weekend homework or set it up during the week.

- If you choose to use *Problem of the Week* as a weekend homework, you could introduce the problem at the end of the week, on Friday. You could then discuss the children's work after the main teaching of a new topic on the following Monday.
- You may choose to set up *Problem of the Week* during the week and work on it in class. Or set it as homework early in the week and go over it at the end of the week.

UNIT 1

Number snooker

Danielle has set herself some target scores in her game of snooker.
Show how she can make these scores.

Teaching objectives
- multiplying and dividing by 10, 100 and 1000
- finding ways to record a procedure
- looking for alternative solutions

Resources
- PCM 1
- paper
- calculators (optional)

Formative assessment
Can the children multiply and divide by 10, 100 and 1000?

Getting started

Give the children a copy of PCM 1 and a calculator (optional). Explain the rules of the game and explain that snooker balls can bounce off the cushions (walls) around the sides of the table and score by entering a pocket (hole). Make sure that the children understand the methods by which scores are made (it is not necessary for the shots to be correct in terms of angle). Ask them to set out and record the method used by Danielle to score 8000. Ask them to find other ways of reaching the same total.

Key teaching point: The digits in a number move 1, 2 or 3 places to the left when multiplying and 1, 2 or 3 places to the right when dividing by 10, 100 or 1000.

Independent task

Tell the children to find each target score. Ask them to design a method of recording how each one could be made and to look for alternative methods of reaching the same score.

Developing the problem

- Ask children to explain how they made some of the target scores.

  Did anyone find a different way to get that score? Is it possible to divide a number by 1000 without using the ÷1000 pocket? What methods can be used to multiply a number by 1000?

- Invite children to show examples of methods used to record their scores and point out how organized recording using a running record of the total makes it easier to check results and look for alternative solutions, for example:

Ball	*1st rebound*		*2nd rebound*		
8	*× 10*	*80*	*× 100*	*8000*	
4000	*× 2*	*8000*			

- Their next task is to set a challenge of 10 different scores for a partner to make.

FOLLOW-UP

- What are the largest and smallest scores that can be made by a ball rebounding off each cushion once?
- Choose one ball. How many different scores is it possible to make if the ball can only rebound off one cushion? Repeat for two cushions, and so on.

Drawing together

Make sure that the children can see a copy of the PCM. Ask them how a series of scores could be made using only one rebound from a cushion:

100 (10 × 10), 40 (4000 ÷ 100), 6 (60 ÷ 10 or 3 × 2), 1800 (60 × 10 × 3), and so on.

Invite children to list all of the scores possible using only the ×10 cushion, the ÷100 cushion, and so on.

Number snooker

Name ________________________________ PCM 1

You need: paper, calculator (optional)

Danielle has set herself some target scores in her game of snooker.

Show how she can make these scores.

Show your calculations. Set out your work clearly.

Rules

Start with a numbered ball placed anywhere on the snooker table.

Balls must be hit to rebound off the cushions and into a pocket.

A ball may hit a maximum of four cushions.

Calculate the score using the number on the ball and the operations on the cushions.

Targets

an odd number

a number ≥ 1 million

a number ≤ 0·004

6 million 27 000 1·402 60

8000 12 0·06 3500

120 200 000 150 540

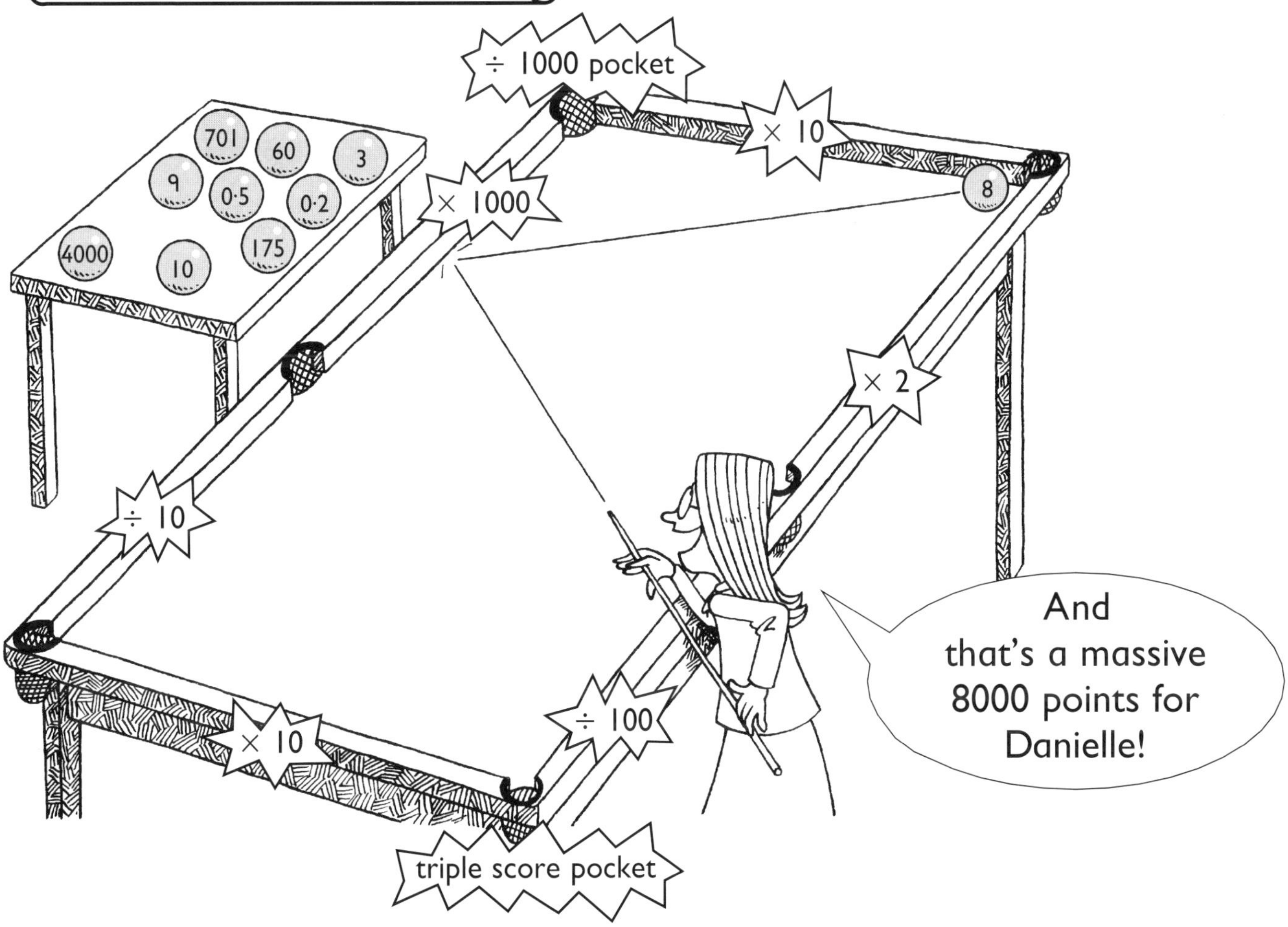

UNIT 2

Stone Age calculators

Teaching objectives

- using factors for multiplication and division
- recognizing patterns and relationships
- presenting alternative solutions

Resources

- PCM 2
- calculators
- paper

Formative assessment

Can the children use factors to calculate multiplication and division problems?

Stone Age calculators allowed only single-digit numbers to be entered. Show how these calculators could be used to solve the neolithic homework problems.

Getting started

Give the children a copy of PCM 2 and explain the problem. Make sure that the children realize that all 2-digit numbers must be entered using factors (for example, $28 \times 14 = (7 \times 4) \times (2 \times 7)$. Ask the children to work with a partner to show how the calculator could be used to double all of the multiples of 10 up to 100. They can jot down the intermediate steps.

Key teaching point: Factors can be used to simplify multiplication and division problems.

Independent task

Tell the children to solve all the homework problems. Tell them to record any examples which have more than one solution and to explain if they think that any of the problems cannot be solved using this calculator.

Developing the problem

- Give the children a calculator. Invite them to explain their solutions to some of the problems and tell the class to check these on a calculator. Ask for alternative solutions to the same problem.
  Does 2 × 9 × 6 × 6 give the same answer as 2 × 2 × 6 × 6? Why? What other solutions are possible?
- Ask the children to explain how they checked their solutions. Their next task is to write some Stone Age homework problems for a partner to solve.

FOLLOW-UP

- Show which problems can still be solved if the 4, 6 and 8 stones are stolen.
- Write a set of subtraction problems to be solved by a partner using the calculator and a subtraction club.

Drawing together

Make a display of the finished work and invite children to explain why certain problems could not be solved using the calculator alone (for example 17×13). Ask children to explain how calculations involving these numbers could be done in stages.

$17 \times 13 =$	10×10	$(2 \times 5 \times 2 \times 5)$	100
	$+10 \times 3$	$(2 \times 5 \times 3)$	$+\ 30$
	$+7 \times 10$	$(7 \times 2 \times 5)$	$+\ 70$
	$+7 \times 3$	(7×3)	$+\ 21$
			221

Ask the children to explore how a series of problems could be solved using factors.

10×6 32×28 20×16 $240 \div 12$ $30 \div 18$ $18 \div 9$ $45 \div 9$

Stone Age calculators

Name ....

PCM 2

You need: a calculator, paper

Stone Age calculators allowed only single-digit numbers to be entered. Show how these calculators could be used to solve the neolithic homework problems.

UNIT 3

Coconut shy

Work out how to score each of the winning totals in this game.

Teaching objectives
- developing multiplication skills
- simplifying a problem
- planning and working methodically

Resources
- PCM 3
- paper
- calculators

Formative assessment
Can the children use pencil and paper methods in multiplication?

Getting started

Give the children a copy of PCM 3 and explain the problem. Ask them to decide if it is possible to score any of the winning totals by hitting a coconut with the 10 ball and missing with the other two balls (it isn't). Tell them to find the winning total that can be made using the 10 ball, the 3 ball and a miss *(10 × 7·2 + 3 × 106 = 390)*.

Key teaching point: Solving the problem is easier if you are able to approximate answers.

Independent task

Tell the children to work on finding each of the totals. Ask them to show all of the calculations used to make each total. Ask them to write an explanation of any strategies that helped them to find the solutions.

Developing the problem

- Ask children to give clues that will help their classmates find the solution to a few of the problems, for example, *90 774* uses just the 3 and the 9 balls; *1323* is scored with only one ball.
- Show the children how to draw up a table of scores that can be made with one ball and add these totals to find scores that can be made with two or three balls, for example:

	Coconut					
Ball	*147*	*3405*	*7942*	*7·2*	*106*	*8951*
3	*441*	*10 215*				
4	*588*					

- Their next task is to find the 10 largest totals that can be scored in this game.

FOLLOW-UP

- Find all the possible scores that can be made using the balls and the two coconuts numbered 3·9 and 8·6.
- Make up a series of winning totals and challenge a partner to work out how to make them.

Drawing together

Ask children to give their solutions to the problems and show their methods of calculation and recording. Draw attention to examples of clear and organized work.

Ask children to explain any strategies they used.

If a winning total ended with a decimal number, what did that tell us about the numbers used to make it? How was 7·2 used to make an integer, 390? What digit would 7·2 × 5 end in? What about 7·2 × 7? ...

Show the children how to use division to check if a number was made with just one ball, for example:

1323 looks like it may have been made with a 9 ball because the digits add up to 9. (1 + 3 + 2 + 3)

$$9\overline{)1323} = 147$$

17 025 ends in a 5 digit so might have been made with the 5 ball.

Coconut shy

Name ....

PCM 3

You need: calculator, paper

Work out how to score each of the winning totals in this game.

Show your calculations. Set out your work clearly.

Winning totals

1323

17 025

57·6

390

1438·2

90 774

116 253

UNIT 4

Can you keep a secret?

Teaching objectives
- working with improper fractions
- comparing fractions and decimals
- selecting mathematics

Resources
- PCM 4
- paper

Formative assessment
Can the children change an improper fraction into a mixed number?

Use the special fraction line to work out the secret message.

Getting started

Give the children a copy of PCM 4 and explain the way the special fraction line can be used to work out the letters in the coded message. (The letters between numbers represent a range of values, for example $0 < r < \frac{1}{4}$.) Ask the children to make lists of fractions that could be used to write the letters *'r'*, *'s'* and *'c'* and to find different ways to write the letter *'i'* using this code.

Key teaching point: Improper fractions can be converted into mixed numbers using multiples of the denominator.

Independent task

Tell the children to solve the secret message. *(there will be a jam party at espionage place. don't spread it.)*

Developing the problem

- Ask children to explain how they solved some of the letters in the message. Ask them to explain how they converted an improper fraction into a mixed number.
- Remind the children how to convert improper fractions into mixed numbers using multiples of the denominator, for example:

$$\frac{16}{6} = \frac{6}{6} + \frac{6}{6} + \frac{4}{6} = 2\frac{4}{6} = 2\frac{2}{3}$$

Show the children how to find equivalent fractions by cancelling, for example:

$$\frac{108 \div 2}{432 \div 2} \bullet \frac{54 \div 2}{216 \div 2} \bullet \frac{27 \div 3}{108 \div 3} \bullet \frac{9 \div 9}{36 \div 9} \bullet = \frac{1}{4}$$

- Their next task is to write a reply to the message.

FOLLOW-UP

- Use the code to write your name and school address.
- Invent your own code using a different fraction number line and challenge a partner to read the message.

Drawing together

Ask children to explain each of the letters used in the message.
Look at examples of work which most clearly show the way in which the problem was solved.
Invite children to challenge the others to decode their replies using the code.

Can you keep a secret?

Name ....

PCM 4

You need: paper

Use the special fraction line to work out the secret message.

Record your work clearly.

z r a s b c i d f g u h j k l m n p q t e v o w x y

$0 \quad \frac{1}{4} \quad \frac{1}{2} \quad \frac{3}{4} \quad 1 \quad 1\frac{1}{5} \quad 1\frac{2}{5} \quad 1\frac{3}{5} \quad 1\frac{4}{5} \quad 2 \quad 2\frac{1}{3} \quad 2\frac{2}{3} \quad 3$

Secret message

$\frac{13}{6} \quad \frac{13}{10} \quad \frac{7}{3} \quad \frac{1}{8} \quad \frac{14}{6} \qquad \frac{14}{5} \quad 0{\cdot}75 \quad \frac{16}{10} \quad \frac{8}{5} \qquad \frac{35}{70} \quad \frac{28}{12} \qquad \frac{16}{64}$

$\frac{28}{20} \quad \frac{36}{144} \quad \frac{20}{12} \qquad 1{\cdot}9 \quad \frac{17}{68} \quad \frac{8}{64} \quad 2{\cdot}2 \quad \frac{29}{7} \qquad \frac{108}{432} \quad \frac{9}{4}$

$\frac{56}{24} \quad \frac{1}{3} \quad \frac{19}{10} \quad \frac{15}{20} \quad \frac{16}{6} \quad \frac{18}{10} \quad \frac{10}{40} \quad 1{\cdot}1 \quad \frac{7}{3} \qquad 1{\cdot}85 \quad \frac{16}{10} \quad \frac{3}{12} \quad 0{\cdot}6 \quad \frac{28}{12}$

$\frac{9}{10} \quad \frac{8}{3} \quad \frac{72}{40} \quad \frac{21}{10} \qquad \frac{4}{12} \quad 1{\cdot}9 \quad 0{\cdot}2 \quad \frac{112}{48} \quad \frac{5}{20} \quad 0{\cdot}8 \qquad \frac{12}{16} \quad \frac{17}{8}$

UNIT 5

Wear & Wave Ltd

Sarah and Joe deliver supplies to the stalls at football matches.
Look at the market research information to work out the minimum numbers of each item that they should deliver to each of these matches.

Teaching objectives
- calculating percentages
- interpreting mathematical information
- communicating clearly

Resources
- PCM 5
- calculators
- paper

Formative assessment
Can the children calculate percentages using mental, written and calculator methods?

Getting started

Give the children a copy of PCM 5 and explain the problem. Ask the children to explain why it is important for people selling goods at sports events to know how many of an item they are likely to sell. Ask them to calculate mentally the numbers of items sold to children in the class, for example:
If 50% of you bought hats / 10% of you bought scarves / 20% bought flags, how many would the class have bought? (all results should be rounded where appropriate)
How much money would be taken if 20% bought flags?

Key teaching point: Multiples of 10% can be used to calculate percentages such as 20% and 30% mentally.

Independent task

Tell the children to investigate how many of each item they should deliver. Ask them to record the information needed to solve each calculation. Ask them to show where they used mental, written or calculator methods to calculate and check each part of the problem.

Developing the problem

- Ask children to explain how they calculated the numbers of items needed for one of the matches. Discuss the children's different approaches to the same calculation and show how these can be used to check solutions. Show how to check the answers by finding 100% of the original number, for example:
  10% of 39 000 = 3900 *90% of 39 000 = 35 100*
  10% + 90% = 100% *3900 + 35 100 = 39 000*
- Their next task is to calculate the amount of money likely to be spent on each item at each match.

FOLLOW-UP

- Look for details of attendance at matches reported in the newspapers. Use the market research data to calculate likely sales at these events.
- Wear & Wave Limited make 13p profit on two out of every three items sold. Calculate their approximate profits for each match.

Drawing together

Ask children to show their work and draw their attention to examples which are set out clearly.

Ask the children to think about what else the data might tell them, for example, what other items might be popular with supporters.

Wear & Wave Ltd

Name ....

You need: calculator, paper

Sarah and Joe deliver supplies to the stalls at football matches.

Look at the market research information to work out the minimum numbers of each item that they should deliver to each of these matches.

Show your calculations. Set out your work clearly.

	Aug–Nov	Dec	Jan–May	Cup Final
Scarf	15%	20%	5%	55%
Hat	10%	25%	15%	40%
Flag	10%	22%	12%	30%
Shirt	45%	35%	2%	80%
Hands	1%	10%	2%	20%

UNIT 6

All the fun of the fair

Teaching objectives
- solving problems using a calculator
- solving problems involving probability
- deciding what information is relevant

Resources
- PCM 6
- calculators
- paper

Formative assessment
Can the children use a calculator to solve realistic problems?

Wetneck Primary School need to raise £9000 to fix the holes in the roof.
They decide to have a school fair to raise the money.
Look at the plans and work out if they are likely to reach their target.

Getting started

Give the children a copy of PCM 6 and explain the problem. Ask the children to work with a partner to calculate the number of people who might be expected to attend the fair and to suggest what the entrance fee should be.

Key teaching point: A calculator is only effective if the person using it knows what type of calculation is needed and how the answer given should be interpreted.

Independent task

Tell the children to investigate the problem by looking at the amounts of money that are likely to be made by each part of the fair, and how the suggestions could be improved. Ask them to record all of the calculations used to reach their conclusion.

Developing the problem

- Invite children to explain their findings and show how they have recorded their calculations relating to certain parts of the fair.
- Show the children how to calculate the likelihood of people winning on the 'Pick a card' game.

  The chances of picking a black card can be worked out as $\frac{26}{52}$ or $\frac{1}{2}$ because there are 26 black cards in the pack of 52 cards.
  If 712 people had two goes each, that's 1424 goes with a 0·5 chance of winning 60p.
  $0{\cdot}5 \times 1424 \times 60p = £427.20$ paid out in prize money.
  So last year 712 people paid $1424 \times 50p = £712$ and about £427.20 was paid back to people who picked a black card.
- Help the children to work out about how much was paid to people who drew a heart.
- Their next task is to suggest what changes could be made to make different events in the fair more profitable.

FOLLOW-UP

- Predict the amount of money that the school is likely to make from the fair. Show how you calculated this figure.
- Show how the children at your school could raise £15 000 from a sponsored event.

Drawing together

Invite children to explain their findings.
Ask the children to explain how to use the calculator to find: the amount you'd need to charge for admission to raise approximately $\frac{1}{3}$ of the money needed; the cost of buying 1 litre of lemonade / 1 bread roll / 1 burger, and so on.

All the fun of the fair

Name ....

PCM 6

You need: calculator, paper

Wetneck Primary School need to raise £9000 to fix the holes in the roof.

They decide to have a school fair to raise the money.

Look at the plans and work out if they are likely to reach their target.

Show your calculations. Set out your work clearly.

NOTICEBOARD

Attendances at recent school fairs:
last year: 712
other years: 652, 680, 732

ADMISSION FEE
£13.00?
We usually only charge 25p.

SOAK THE TEACHER
170 people had a go last year.
Was **40p** a go.
Will they pay **£53** a go?

Pick a card. 50p a go.

Heart wins £1
Black card wins 60p
Everyone had 2 goes last year!

Two-dice roll
40p a go

Roll 2 of any number to win £1.
Everyone played at least 6 times in recent years.

Cake stall
We usually have about 70 cakes. I'm sure we can sell them for at least £2000.
What do you think?

BURGERS
Every year we sell 600 at 70p each. We buy the bread rolls at £1.80 for 4 and boxes of 6 burgers for £2.28. Sauce, salad and so on costs about £12 for the whole fair.

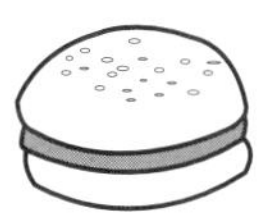

DRINKS
We sold 500 cups at 20p each last year. Each cup holds 400 ml. We bought 60 litres of lemonade for £29.

UNIT 7

Goal scorers

Use the bar charts to find which of these hockey players and teams are best at scoring goals.

Teaching objectives
- interpreting bar charts
- finding averages
- communicating results

Resources
- PCM 7
- paper

Formative assessment
Can the children use the information contained in a bar chart to describe a situation?

Getting started

Give the children a copy of PCM 7 and explain the problem. Ask the children to answer some specific questions using the bar charts, for example:

In how many matches has Howard scored 2 goals? How many goals has Walsom scored? How many goals have Blakely scored? Which team has the best goal-scoring average? How many goals per match is the mode for Gibbs?

Key teaching point: Averages provide a useful way of comparing facts and figures.

Independent task

Tell the children to write a list of as many facts and figures as they can find out about each player and to explain how they worked out the information from the graphs. Suggest that they draw graphs to show some of their findings. Ask them to record any calculations used.

Developing the problem

- Ask children to read out some of the facts and figures and show any graphs drawn.
- Ask the children to explain what sort of average is used in the section on the PCM entitled 'average number of goals per game'. Explain that you need to know the number of matches played in order to work out the mean average of goals per game for each team. Show them how to work out the number of matches played using trial and improvement.
  Branstead scored 46 goals with an average of 2·3 goals per game
  46 goals in 46 games would be 46 ÷ 46 = 1
  46 goals in 23 games would be 46 ÷ 23 = 2
  46 goals in 10 games would be 46 ÷ 10 = 4·6
  46 goals in 20 games would be 46 ÷ 20 = 2·3
- Their next task is to work out the mean number of goals per game scored by each player.

FOLLOW-UP

- Work out the average number of days per week you were at school last month.
- Collect information that can be presented in graphs and used to compare players in other sports.

Drawing together

Ask children to show their work. Look at examples of graphs which make it easy to compare the different players.

Show children where they could have referred to the range, mean, median and mode of the data, for example:

What was the range of the number of goals scored by the different teams? What is the mean number of goals per game for Walsom? What is the median number of goals per game scored by the different players? Which players do you think might play for which teams?

Goal scorers

Name ....

PCM 7

You need: paper

Use the bar charts to find which of these hockey players and teams are best at scoring goals and which players are in which teams.

Set out your work clearly on paper.

Goal-scoring record: Players

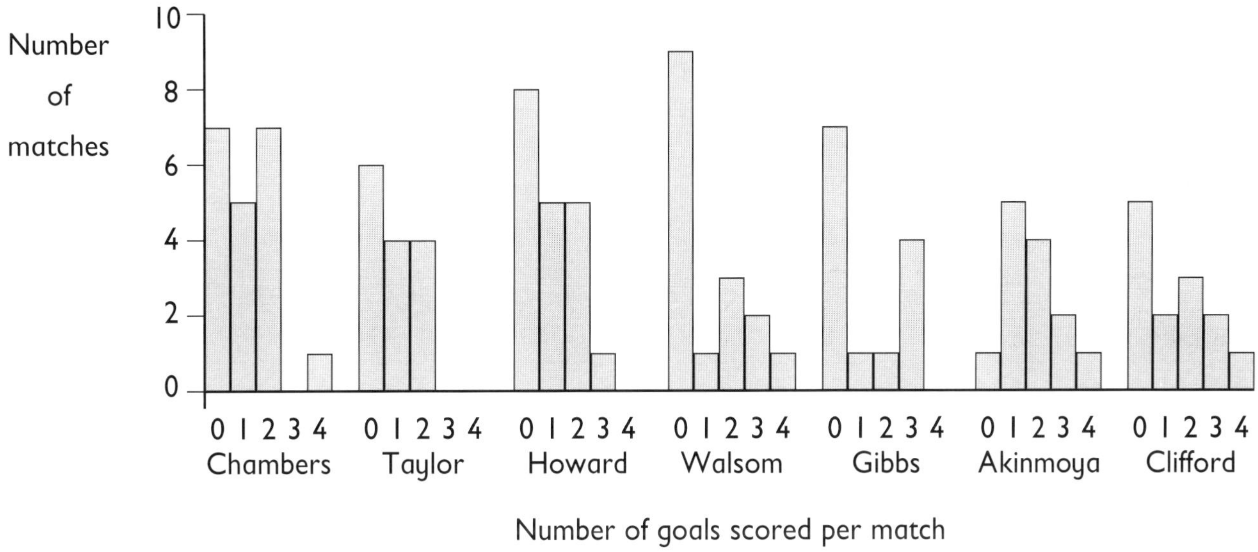

Goal-scoring record: Teams

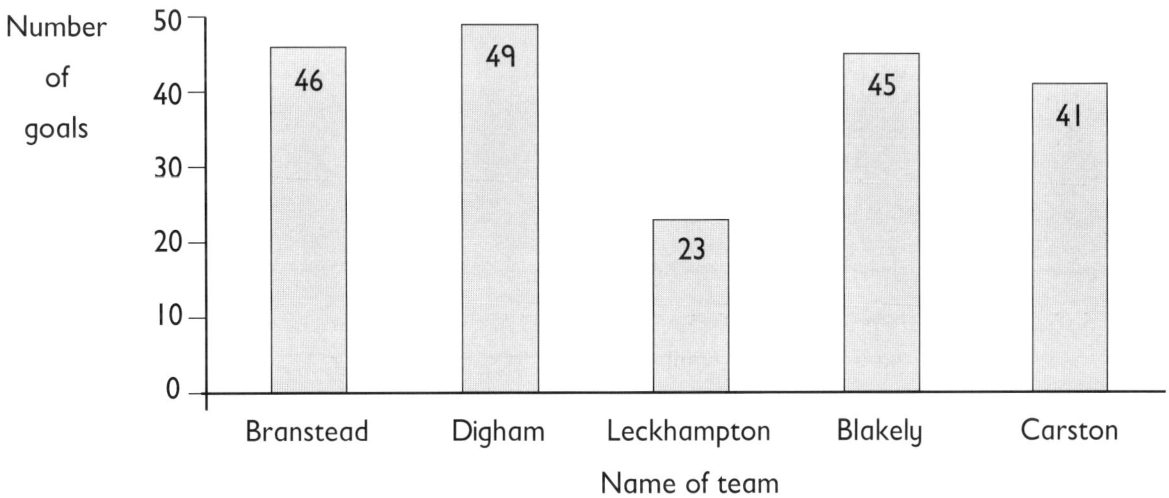

All teams have played the same number of games but players may have played less.

Average number of goals per game	
Blakely	2·25
Carston	2·05
Branstead	2·30
Digham	2·45
Leckhampton	1·15

UNIT 8

Video-link homework conferencing

Teaching objectives
- solving shape puzzles
- simplifying a problem
- looking for patterns

Resources
- PCM 8
- skipping ropes or string
- paper

Formative assessment
Do the children understand how simplifying a problem can help to solve it?

A new system of cables and computers will connect the homes of 10 children in your class. Each cable connects 2 homes. Work out how many cables will be needed to complete the system.

Getting started

Give the children a copy of PCM 8 and explain the problem. Use rope or string to demonstrate how many cables will be needed to connect 4 people. Ask one of the children to sit down, and then discuss how many cables are no longer needed. Repeat so there are only 2 children left.

Key teaching point: Difficult problems can often be solved by looking at the solutions to simpler versions of the same problem.

Independent task

Tell the children to investigate connecting 10 children. Ask them to record their work so that it can be easily checked by someone looking for proof that their solution is correct. Ask them to include any drawings or diagrams used.

Developing the problem

- Ask children to explain how they would work out how many cables are needed to connect 6 children. Repeat for numbers up to 10 children. Look at examples of diagrams used and ask children to explain how they know they counted the number of cables accurately.
- Show the children how to arrange their findings in a table and use this to search for a pattern in the results.

Number of children	*Number of cables*
4	*6*
5	*10*

- Their next task is to work out the cost of the system if cables cost £99.97 each, assuming everyone has already been given a computer.

FOLLOW-UP

- Work out how many cables would be needed to connect everyone in your school.
- Draw a graph that can be used to show the numbers of cables needed to connect different numbers of children.

Drawing together

Invite children to complete a table showing the numbers of cables needed for groups of children ranging in size between 2 and 10 and ask them to suggest the numbers of cables needed to connect the whole class based on their findings. Ask children to explain any patterns they see in the table, and to suggest ways of finding how many cables might be needed to connect any number of children.

Video-link homework conferencing

Name ....

PCM 8

You need: paper

A new system of cables and computers will connect the homes of 10 children in your class. Each cable connects 2 homes.

Work out how many cables will be needed to complete the system.

Set out your work clearly.

UNIT 9

Chimp on a tricycle

The chimp-on-a-tricycle toy can be programmed to draw a closed shape.
Find the total length it must travel to draw each shape.

Teaching objectives
- converting smaller to larger units of length and *vice versa*
- modelling a problem
- looking for alternative solutions

Resources
- PCM 9
- cm-squared paper

Formative assessment
Can the children use standard metric units and relationships?

Getting started

Give the children a copy of PCM 9 and a piece of cm-squared paper. Explain the way in which the toy moves and ask the children to plot the pattern made by the chimp using the length inputs *1 square, 3 squares, 3 squares*, repeat. Make sure that the children start drawing from a point near the centre of the paper. Ask the children to measure the length of the lines of the resulting closed shape. Point out that they must work out how far the chimp travels, not just the perimeter, each time. The shape is closed when the pencil returns to the original starting point before repeating its original course.

Key teaching point: Squared paper can be used to scale-model problems involving much larger measurements.

Independent task

Tell the children to use cm-squared paper to help them find the distances for each of the patterns. Explain that these drawings should also be used in the presentation of their finished work. Point out that they have to convert some of the distances into different units.

Developing the problem

- Show the children how a repeating pattern of *3 metres, 6 metres, 9 metres*, can be modelled as *3 cm-squares, 6 cm-squares, 9 cm-squares*, on squared paper and how the length of the pattern in centimetres can be converted into metres.
- Show the children how to follow the instructions accurately by rotating the paper and always drawing in the same direction: start near the centre of the paper, draw a line 3 squares long going straight away from your body, turn the paper a quarter turn to the right, draw a line going 6 squares away from your body, turn the paper a quarter turn to the right, and so on.
- Make a display of the different patterns made by the children and point out those which are correct.
- Their next task is to find the length of each pattern if each cm-square represents 1 kilometre.

FOLLOW-UP

- Find out what patterns are made if the chimp is given three different even-number lengths to follow.
- Find other patterns that the chimp can make.

Drawing together

Complete the display of the chimp-patterns. Ask children to explain how they calculated the lengths of each pattern.
Show the children how to use perimeters of shapes within the patterns to calculate some of the lengths: the *1-3-5-repeat* pattern makes four identical rectangles and a square. If you find the perimeter of one of the rectangles, you can multiply that length by 4 and add it to the perimeter of the square to get the total distance travelled.

Chimp on a tricycle

Name ....

PCM 9

You need: squared paper

The chimp-on-a-tricycle toy can be programmed to draw a closed shape.

Find the total length it must travel to draw each shape.

Set out your work clearly.

Chimp's Instructions

Forward length ______________

Left turn 90 degrees

Forward length ______________

Left turn 90 degrees

Forward length ______________

Left turn 90 degrees

Repeat

Find the distances travelled using these input lengths:

1 1 cm, 3 cm, 3 cm

2 1 m, 3 m, 3 m

3 1 km, 3 km, 5 km

4 1 m, 3 m, 5 m

5 3 m, 6 m, 9 m

6 3 cm, 6 cm, 9 cm

UNIT 10

Glenda's global restaurant

Teaching objectives
- comparing different times around the world
- recording work systematically
- modelling a problem

Resources
- PCM 10
- paper

Formative assessment
Can the children devise systems to calculate and record their answers?

Glenda works in London and uses a computer to cook the meals for her fully-automated global restaurants.
Use the information to work out cooking timetables for each of the restaurants.

Getting started

Give the children a copy of PCM 10 and explain that the meals are cooked in each of the different branches of the restaurant when the ovens are switched on from London by remote control. Explain that Glenda needs to know when to activate the ovens to cook each of the different parts of the meal. Ask the children to draw up a timetable showing when the different parts of the meal should be cooked for the London and Brussels restaurants.

Key teaching point: Complex problems can be simplified using diagrams and flow charts.

Independent task

Tell the children to produce clear timetables showing the times in London at which Glenda needs to activate the ovens. Tell them to keep copies of any diagams or drawings that they used to help model the problem.

Developing the problem

- Invite children to complete a timetable showing when the ovens should be activated for the London restaurant. Ask children to explain how these timings can be used to work out the timings for the Athens restaurant.
- Invite them to share any methods used to model these problems.
- Show the children how to use number lines to model the problem:

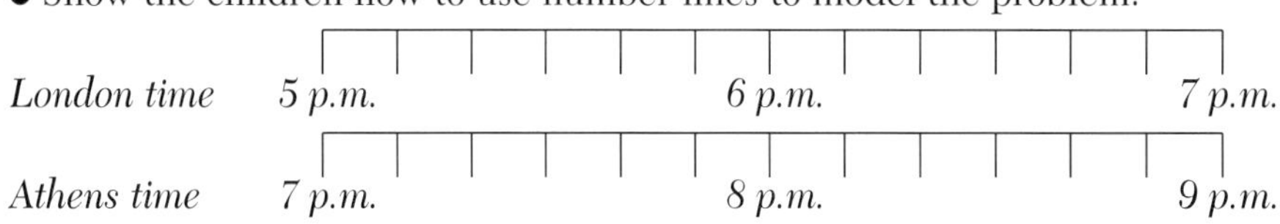

- Their next task is to calculate the activation times if all of the meals were to be served 75 minutes later.

FOLLOW-UP

- Work out the cooking times for a different meal and draw up a new timetable.
- Imagine that branches of Glenda's global restaurants opened in other cities around the world. Work out the time difference and calculate the cooking timetables.

Drawing together

Invite children to show their work and explain how they solved the problems. Look at examples of timetables that clearly show the information required.
Ask the children to explain how answers to one part of the problem might be used to find other answers.
Ask the children to explain when Glenda might telephone different branches to ask the diners what they thought of the meal:
When would be a good time for Glenda to phone Athens/Tokyo to ask what people thought of the fish soup/apple pie? What time would that be in London?

Glenda's global restaurant

Name ....

You need: paper

Glenda works in London and uses a computer to cook the meals for her fully-automated global restaurants.

Use the information to work out cooking timetables for each of the restaurants.

All meals must be served at these local times.

Starter	8:30 p.m.
Main Course	9:10 p.m.
Dessert	9:50 p.m.

Today's Menu		Cooking time
Starter	Fish soup	62 minutes
Main Course	Chicken	85 minutes
	Chips	11 minutes
	Carrots	22 minutes
Dessert	Apple pie	24 minutes
	Custard	8 minutes

Glenda's Global Restaurant branches

– 5 hours	GMT	+ 1 hour	+ 2 hours	+ 9 hours	+ 10 hours
Washington DC	London	Brussels	Athens	Tokyo	Canberra

UNIT 11

Aristotle the arithmetic aardvark

Teaching objectives
- adding and subtracting pairs of numbers
- exploring problems and recording work systematically
- devising procedures

Resources
- PCM 11
- paper

Formative assessment
Can the children add and subtract accurately, using mental strategies and written methods where appropriate?

Aristotle uses the numbers on the apples to calculate a series of target numbers.
He only uses addition and subtraction, and he never uses the same apple twice in any calculation.
Show which of his numbers can be made in more than seven different ways.

Getting started

Give the children a copy of PCM 11 and explain the problem. Ask them to explain how it is possible to produce target numbers where the last digit is *1* or *9* *(by adding or subtracting 9 from a multiple of 10)*. Tell them to find all the numbers that can be made using the 400 apple and just one other.

Key teaching point: Mental strategies are the most appropriate methods to use when adding or subtracting multiples of 9 or 10.

Independent task

Tell the children to find each of the target numbers. Ask them to record each solution clearly and make notes on any strategies used to solve the problems.

Developing the problem

- Ask children to show their methods of recording and to explain their strategies.
- Display one of the target numbers and invite children to list their solutions to that problem.
- Show the children how solutions can be adapted to make other solutions.
  10 000 – 9000 = 1000
  1000 + 500 + 70 = 1570
- Their next task is to find different ways to make a new target number, *1*.

FOLLOW-UP

- Find the different target numbers that can be made using only three apples.
- Solve a chain of targets, for example *14 000, 291, 109, –60, 159*, moving from each target to the next using the numbers on the apples.

Can anyone think of a different solution to that problem?

Drawing together

Tell the children to record all the solutions with a list of the target numbers.
Ask the children to set each other chains of targets.

Which target numbers can still be made if the numbers on the apples are multiplied by 10?

Aristotle the arithmetic aardvark

Name ....

PCM 11

You need: paper

Aristotle uses the numbers on the apples to calculate a series of target numbers.

He only uses addition and subtraction, and he never uses the same apple twice in any calculation.

Show which of his numbers can be made in more than seven different ways. Show your calculations. Set out your work clearly.

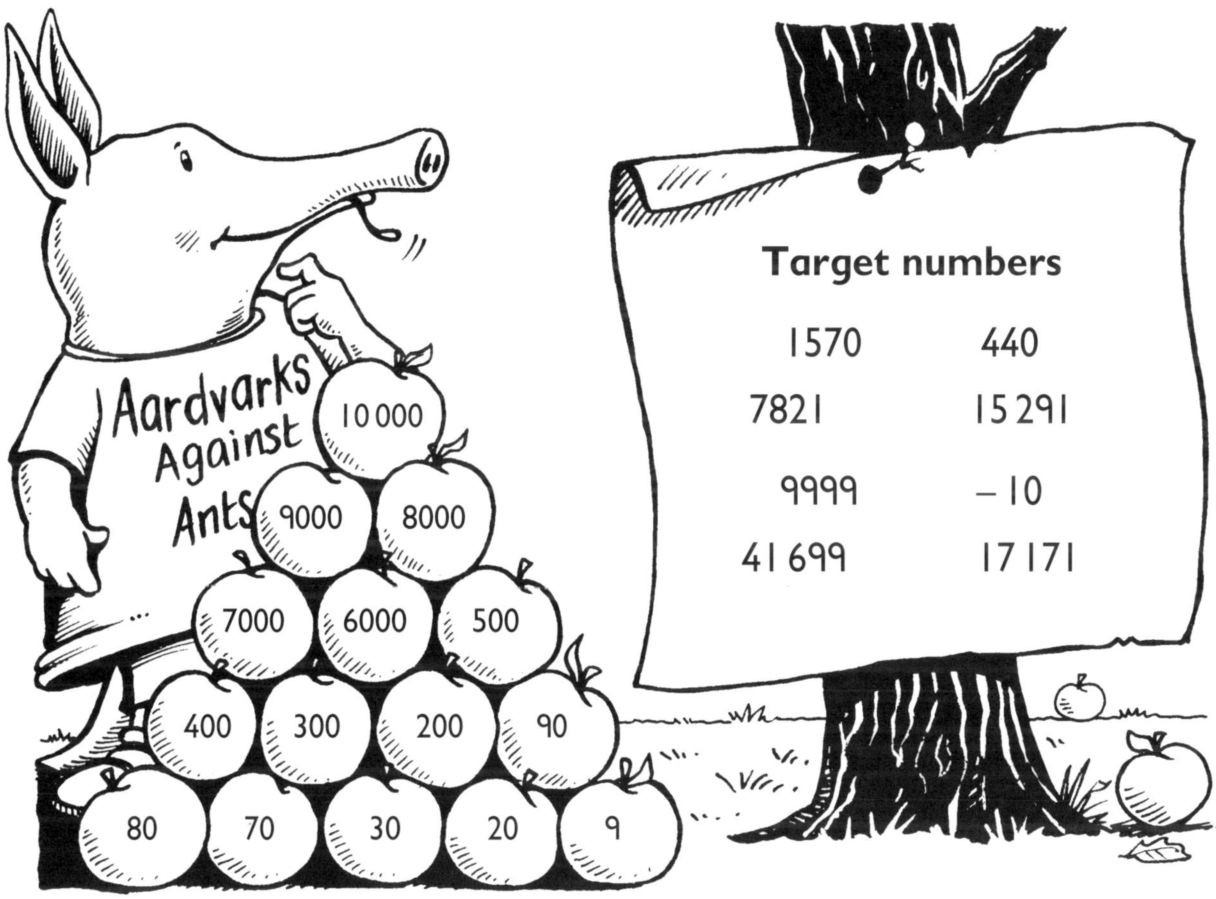

UNIT 12

Squares and tables

Kenji uses a table to work out the totals in this sequence of squares.
Complete the table and find a way to work out the totals.

Teaching objectives
- extending number sequences and patterns
- recognizing patterns and relationships
- making and testing hypotheses

Resources
- PCM 12
- paper

Formative assessment
Can the children recognize patterns and describe relationships?

Getting started

Give the children a copy of PCM 12 and look at the sequence of squares. Ask the children to find the totals for squares 4 and 5 and to draw squares 6 and 7.

Key teaching point: Organizing data in a tabular form can help to make the patterns in number sequences easier to identify.

Independent task

Ask the children to keep a record of any patterns they noticed and to record all the methods that they tried. Explain that they should complete the table and use it to look for patterns in the totals in order to find a way to allow them to calculate the total for any square in the sequence.

Developing the problem

- Invite children to describe any patterns they noticed. Show the children how to mark these on the table, as shown.
- Invite children to explain their methods and discuss how to test them using the totals on the table, for example:
  For each new square 1 add on 8.
- Their next task is to investigate a sequence of squares using multiples of 3.

Square	*Total*
1	*4*
	+8
2	*12*
	+8
3	*20*

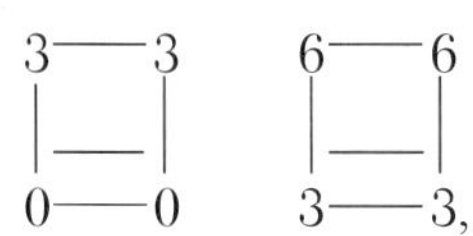

, and so on.

FOLLOW-UP

- Investigate a series of squares using multiples of 4 or 9, and so on.
- Investigate a series of triangles using multiples of 5 or 7.

Drawing together

Invite children to explain any lessons they have learned about solving this type of problem.
Children may have noticed that the total for the third square is $(3 \times 8) - 4$, and for the fourth square it is $(4 \times 8) - 4$. Encourage them to explain why it is necessary to subtract *4* each time.

Squares and tables

Name ....

PCM 12

You need: paper

Kenji uses a table to work out the totals in this sequence of squares.

Complete the table and find a way to work out the totals.

Record your work clearly.

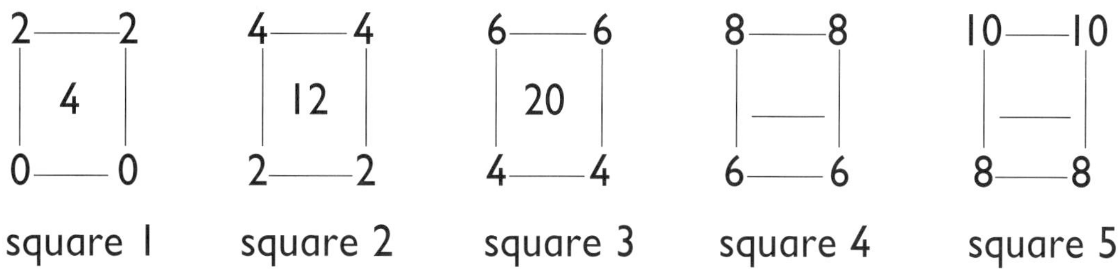

Square	Total
1	4
2	12
3	20
4	
5	
6	
7	
8	
9	
10	
30	

UNIT 13

Overdrawn at the bank

The singers in the band 'The Rockefellaz' have spent too much money.
Work out the amount of money owed by each person.

Teaching objectives
- working with negative numbers in context
- using trial and improvement methods
- planning and working methodically

Resources
- PCM 13
- calculators (optional)
- paper

Formative assessment
Can the children work systematically to solve a problem using trial and improvement?

Getting started

Give the children a copy of PCM 13 and ask the children to use the information provided to produce two lists, headed *What we know* and *What we need to know*. Point out that the band members are paid £65 each day and explain that they will have been paid 13 times more after the statement on the 1st March. Ask the children to work out this total (£845).

Key teaching point: When using trial and improvement methods, it helps to use a system for recording unsuccessful attempts at finding a solution.

Independent task

Ask children to suggest methods they will use to find out who owes each amount. Explain that they will need to be very organized and will find it useful to record all of their attempted solutions when using a trial and improvement approach. Tell them to investigate the problem. Most children will need to use a calculator.

Developing the problem

- Invite children to explain their methods and findings.
- Show the children how to begin by choosing a band member they know a lot about, for example, they know that Kevyn had £69 and was paid £845. He would have had £914 if he hadn't spent any money. They know he spent lots on clothes (probably £3121) but not much on other things. They might guess that he owed the smallest amount (£38 577). So they could try adding £3121 and some of the smaller totals, then subtracting £914 to find how much he owed. For example: *(£35 195 + £415 + £3121 + £678) − £914 = £38 495 owed.*
- Explain that this is not the correct answer but should be recorded as it gets us closer to the correct answer.
- Their next task is to work out how long it would take each member of the band to repay their debt at a rate of £65 per day.

FOLLOW-UP

- The bank charges £150 for every £9000 an account is overdrawn. How much does each person owe now?
- The record company agree to repay each overdraft at a rate of £17 500 per week. Show a weekly record of repayments for each account.

Drawing together

Show the children how a table could be used to record trial and error attempts:

Kevyn

Income	*clothes*	*house*	*car*	*holiday*	***amount owed***	
£914	*£3121*	*£35 195*	*£415*	*£678*	***£38 495***	✗
£914	*£3121*	*£35 195*	*£415*	*£760*	***£38 577***	✓

Ask the children to explain any methods that helped them to solve this problem.

Overdrawn at the bank

Name ....

PCM 13

You need: a calculator (optional), paper

The singers in the band 'The Rockefellaz' have spent too much money.

Work out the amount of money owed by each person.

MCD Bank
21 Bank lane
Farthington

Bank Statement
1st March

Dear Rockefellaz,

You now each have:

Davy	£2532
Wavy	£1920
Sharyn	£1506
Kevyn	£69

(includes £65 per person paid on 1st March.)

MCD Bank
21 Bank lane
Farthington

14th March

Dear Rockefellaz,

You now owe £1 115 788.

Account holder 1	owes £38 577
Account holder 2	owes £217 754
Account holder 3	owes £673 594
Account holder 4	owes £185 863

(Includes £65 per person paid on 14th March.)

Things we have bought

Houses	Cars	Clothes	Holidays
£213 000	£415	£675	£760
£35 195	£13 000	£21	£8456
£444 999	£17 656	£490	£214
£174 250	£13 265	£3121	£678

UNIT 14

Cuddly toys

Is it possible to win the cuddly toys in this game?

Teaching objectives
- using mental strategies
- explaining strategies
- looking for alternative solutions

Resources
- PCM 14
- paper

Formative assessment
Can the children explain different solutions to a mental calculation?

Getting started

Give the children a copy of PCM 14 and explain the rules of the darts game. Ask them to predict if it will be possible to win any of the toys in this game. Record predictions and ask children to briefly explain their reasoning. Tell the children to record different ways to score 1400.

Key teaching point: Calculations such as 200×6 can be solved using mental approaches such as $2 \times 6 \times 100$ or 2×600.

Independent task

Tell the children to investigate if any of the toys can be won, and if so, how. Ask them to record each solution and to write notes about the different strategies they used in the investigation. Point out that one or two of the darts might miss (and thus score zero), and that more than one dart can land in the same section of the dartboard.

Developing the problem

- Ask children to list different solutions to some of the scores and compare their findings with their original predictions.
- Ask children to explain the mental methods used to solve some of the calculations and make sure that they can use a variety of approaches, for example:
  $170 \times 6 = (100 \times 6) + (70 \times 6)$
  or $(10 \times 6) + (7 \times 6) \times 10$
  or $170 \times 2 \times 3$ *and so on.*
- Their next task is to add four more cuddly toys to the list of prizes. Two of the toys should have a score that can be made in 10 different ways and two should have a score that cannot.

FOLLOW-UP

- Find the 10 largest and smallest scores possible when one dart lands in the double ring, one dart in the $\times 6$ ring and one dart in the $\times 7$ ring.
- Find all of the scores over 900 that can be made with a single dart.

Drawing together

Ask children to show their work and explain their methods for recording. Draw attention to examples which are clear and well organized and explain how this makes checking easier and helps in the search for additional solutions.
Show the children how parts of one solution can be used in other solutions, for example:
Target 1400
$(200 \times 6) + (200 \times 1) + 0 = 1400$
$(200 \times 6) + (100 \times 2) + 0 = 1400$
$(200 \times 6) + (100 \times 1) + (100 \times 1) = 1400$ *and so on.*

Cuddly toys

Name ....

You need: paper

Is it possible to win the cuddly toys in this game?

Show your calculations. Set out your work clearly.

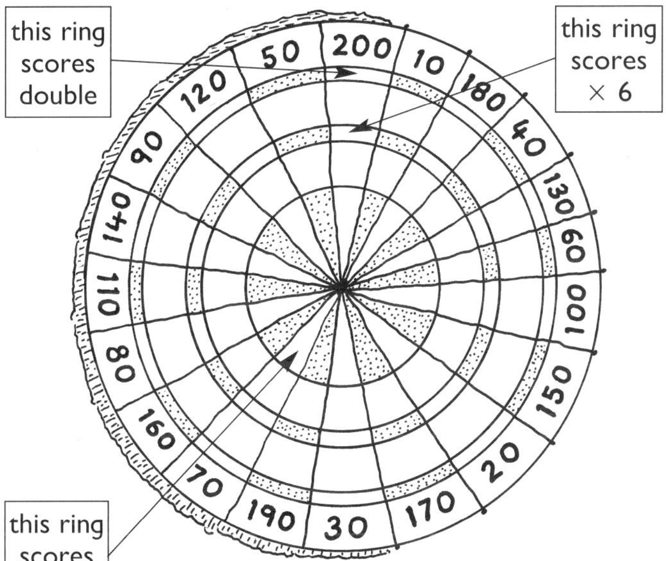

rules

Throw 3 darts to score the total on the toy.
Each total must be scored 10 different ways to win the toy.
All misses score zero.

UNIT 15

Cargo ships

Teaching objectives

- solving multiplication and division problems
- deciding what information is relevant
- planning and working methodically

Resources

- PCM 15
- paper

Formative assessment

Can the children decide what information is necessary to complete the problem?

Each ship has a different number of cargo bays.
All of the bays hold the same quantity of sand when full.
All of the ships should be full but they have been loaded with the wrong amounts.
Work out what should be done to make sure the correct cargoes are delivered.

Getting started

Give the children a copy of PCM 15 and read through the problem. Tell them to discuss the problem with a partner and to use colouring pencils to highlight the information that is needed to complete the task. They should highlight the cargo in tonnes, the sand left behind, the number of bays, and whether they are full, half-full or empty. The destination and position are irrelevant. Invite children to list the information they have selected.

Key teaching point: Deciding upon which information is relevant is an important stage in problem solving.

Independent task

Tell the children to record a list of the information they thought relevant to work out each cargo, and to explain their solution in a step by step account.

Developing the problem

- Invite children to explain some of the stages of their solutions.
  What was one of the first things we needed to know? Why was that important? How did you work that out?
- Demonstrate how to find out how much a cargo bay holds:
  Arch has a cargo of 1 805 000 kilograms when full. It has 13 full bays and 6 empty bays, which makes a total of 19 bays.
  We divide 1 805 000 kilograms by 19 to find how much sand each one holds, which is 95 000 kilograms.
- Their next task is to write instructions explaining which ships need to return to the dock and how much sand needs to be loaded on each.

FOLLOW-UP

- Make up a similar problem where each of the bays holds 57 000 kilograms. Challenge a partner to solve it.
- Use an atlas to work out the routes taken by each ship. If each ship travelled 86 kilometres every 8 hours, approximately how long would each journey take?

Drawing together

Invite children to show their solutions to the problems.

Cargo ships

Name ....

PCM 15

You need: paper

Each ship has a different number of cargo bays.

All of the bays hold the same quantity of sand when full.

All of the ships should be full but they have been loaded with the wrong amounts.

Work out what should be done to make sure the correct cargoes are delivered.

Document 1:	**Schedule**	
Ship	*Destination*	*Cargo when full in kilograms*
Ark	Hull	
Art	Singapore	
Artemis	Riga	
Arch	New York	1 805 000
Aries	Lisbon	2 090 000
Archer	Naples	1 710 000

Document 2:	**Captain's radio reports**			
Ship	*Bays*			*Position*
Arch	13 full		6 empty	At sea
Artemis	12 full		0 empty	At sea
Art	14 full		0 empty	At sea
Aries	7 full	14 half full	1 empty	At sea
Archer	9 full	6 half full	3 empty	At sea
Ark	13 full		0 empty	At sea

UNIT 16

Congratulations: You've won a holiday!

Hollie has won a holiday.
Look at the information to help her find out where her spending money will buy the most.

Teaching objectives
- converting pounds sterling to foreign currency
- devising procedures
- explaining reasoning

Resources
- PCM 16
- calculators
- paper

Formative assessment
Can the children select appropriate methods for their calculations?

Getting started

Give the children a copy of PCM 16 and discuss the problem. Explain that exchange rates are used to convert money into different currencies. Ask the children to work with a partner to convert £500 into each of the different currencies.

Key teaching point: Modelling a problem and making sure it is understood is the first step towards solving it.

Independent task

Tell the children to investigate where Hollie's money will buy most. Explain that they should set out their findings so that different costs can be compared. Tell them to include explanations of how pounds can be converted into the different currencies.

Developing the problem

- Ask children to explain how the £375 spending money can be converted into the different currencies.
- Show them how to convert £375 into Jamaican dollars:
  £375 = £300 + £50 + £25
  £100 = 6300 dollars so £300 = 6300 × 3 = 18 900 dollars
  £50 = 6300 dollars ÷ 2 = 3150 dollars
  £25 = 6300 dollars ÷ 4 = 1575 dollars
  23 625 dollars
  or 6300 × 3·75 = 23 625 dollars
- Show the children how to work out how to convert £1 into each currency, for example: ***£100 = 16 416·75 Japanese yen so £1 = 16 416·75 ÷ 100 = 164·1675 yen.***
- Their next task is to find the approximate cost in pounds for a meal and a drink in each country.

FOLLOW-UP

- Convert other prices and values into foreign currencies, for example pocket money in US dollars, school dinner money in Japanese yen, favourite chocolate in New Zealand dollars and so on.
- Look in the newspaper or on the internet to find exchange rates for other currencies. Convert £375 into these currencies.

Drawing together

Invite children to show their work and explain which country they believe will offer the best value. Ask children to explain how they made decisions about rounding answers.
Show the children how converting to pounds can help when comparing prices, for example:

cost of drink					
Syria	*50 pounds*	÷	*3357.8 pounds/pound sterling*	=	*74.45 pence*
US	*1·5 dollars*	÷	*1·5 dollars / pound*	=	*£1*

Congratulations: You've won a holiday!

Name ....

PCM 16

You need: a calculator, paper

Hollie has won a holiday.

Look at the information to help her find out where her spending money will buy the most.

SUPER HOLIDAYS

Dear Hollie
Congratulations.
You've won a holiday and £375 spending money!
Just choose one of these destinations.
We've included details about costs to help you decide where to go.

GOOD VIEW HOLIDAYS

Destination	Exchange rates		
Jamaica	£100 =	6300	dollars
Japan	£100 =	16 416·75	yen
New Zealand	£50 =	164·63	dollars
Syria	£50 =	3357·8	pounds
United States	£10 =	15	dollars

FLY-ME HOLIDAYS

Approximate prices

	drink	*lunch*	*jeans*	*CD*	*souvenir*	*cinema*	*T-shirt*
Jamaica	95	150	1000	400	300	250	200
Japan	400	1400	7000	2000	1300	1000	1800
New Zealand	6·50	20	80	30	14	13	28
Syria	50	120	670	270	200	540	200
United States	1·5	8	50	13	12·5	6	17

UNIT 17

Fractions in an 'L'

The children arranged sets of fraction cards in a repeating L-shaped pattern on a blank 6 by 6 grid. Each L-shaped layer contained just one type of fraction. They also added up the total value of fractions on the grid.
Show how they made each of these totals.

Teaching objectives
- using a calculator to convert fractions to decimals
- planning and working methodically
- using trial and improvement methods

Resources
- PCM 17
- calculators

Formative assessment
Can the children convert fractions into decimals?

Getting started

Give the children a copy of PCM 17 and a calculator and ask them to find the total of the fractions in the L-shape on the grid. Ask them to explain how they could find the total of an L-shape elsewhere on the grid. Explain how the fractions can be converted into decimals, for example $\frac{1}{2} = 1 \div 2 = 0{\cdot}5$, $\frac{3}{4} = 3 \div 4 = 0{\cdot}75$, and so on.

Key teaching point: Converting fractions into decimals can make them easier to compare and work with.

Independent task

Tell the children to investigate the problem. Tell them to record how each of the totals was made and to show how they calculated each answer. You may need to help them realize that there are eleven of each of the five fractions.

Developing the problem

- Invite children to explain how they found the decimal equivalents of each of the fractions. Ask them to arrange these decimals in size order and use this order to help decide what the largest and smallest possible totals must be.
  How many times would the $\frac{3}{4}$ card appear in the largest/smallest total?
  Where does it need to be? What about $\frac{1}{10}$?
- Help children to model the problem by making a grid and fraction cards from pieces of paper marked with both decimal and vulgar fractions.
- Their next task is to find totals that they can challenge a partner to find.

FOLLOW-UP

- Find the smallest and largest totals that can be made by placing cards on the grid in an arrangement where no two cards of the same size meet edge to edge.
- Is it possible to make a total that is a whole number?

Drawing together

Invite children to explain their answers to some of their problems. Look at examples of work which record findings in a clear and organized manner and explain how this helps you to avoid making mistakes and communicates findings most effectively.
Point out the relationship between adding sets of decimals and adding integers, for example:
$0{\cdot}5 + 0{\cdot}5 + 0{\cdot}5 = 1{\cdot}5$
$5 + 5 + 5 = 15$, *and so on.*
Give the children a calculator and ask them to arrange sets of fractions in order of size; for example: $\frac{1}{2}$ $\frac{3}{7}$ $\frac{4}{9}$ $\frac{8}{12}$ $\frac{2}{5}$

Fractions in an 'L'

Name ....

PCM 17

You need: a calculator, paper

The children arranged sets of fraction cards in a repeating L-shaped pattern on a blank 6 by 6 grid.

Each L-shaped layer contained just one type of fraction.

They also added up the total value of fractions on the grid.

Show how they made each of these totals.

UNIT 18

The intersection question

Teaching objectives
- defining and exploring intersecting lines
- working systematically
- presenting results

Resources
- PCM 18
- paper

Formative assessment
Can the children develop organized methods for carrying out work and reporting findings in investigations?

Each of these patterns can be drawn without lifting your pencil from the paper or retracing over any of the lines.
Add the numbers on each intersection you pass through to find the total for each drawing.
Rearrange the numbers on the intersections to make the largest and smallest totals possible for each drawing.

Getting started

Give the children a copy of PCM 18 and explain the problem. Ask them to find out how each shape can be drawn without lifting the pencil or retracing over a line. Ask them to design a set of instructions explaining how to complete one of the drawings.

Key teaching point: A logical approach and an organized record helps to focus effort during investigations.

Independent task

Tell the children to investigate finding the largest and smallest totals for each drawing by rearranging the numbers on the intersections. Explain that they should develop a method of recording how each drawing and each total was made.

Developing the problem

- Invite children to show how some of the drawings and totals are made.
  Did anyone find a different way to complete that drawing?
  Ask children to explain how they organized their work and made sure that they remembered how to complete each drawing.
- Show them how to write a set of instructions for completing the drawings using letters of the alphabet to identify each intersection.
- Their next task is to find all of the totals that can be made with these drawings.

FOLLOW-UP

- Invent your own set of drawings that can be made using the same rules and challenge a partner to find out how they are done.
- Find out which digits and capital letters can be drawn without lifting the pencil or retracing over the lines.

Drawing together

Make a display of the finished work and draw attention to examples that demonstrate an organized approach and give a clear record of how each of the totals was made.
Show the children how to record the number of times the line passes through an intersection when drawing by placing tally marks next to the intersections. This information can then be used to arrange the numbers to make the totals; if a large total is required, the largest numbers are arranged at intersections visited most often.

The intersection question

You need: paper

Each of these patterns can be drawn without lifting your pencil from the paper or retracing over any of the lines.

Add the numbers on each intersection you pass through to find the total for each drawing.

Rearrange the numbers on the intersections to make the largest and smallest totals possible for each drawing.

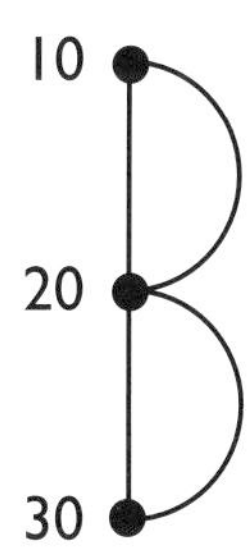

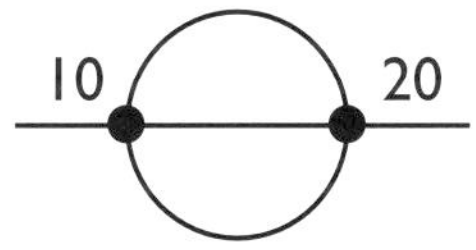

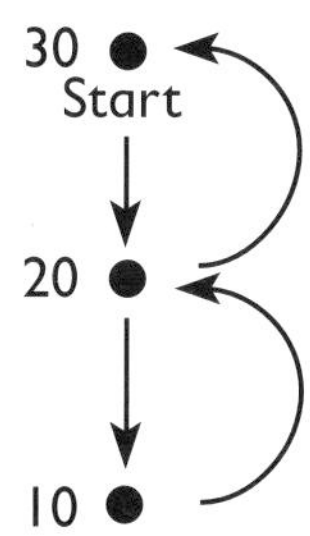

30 + 20 + 10 + 20 + 30 = 110

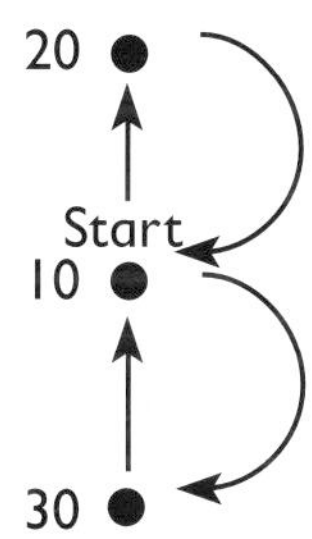

10 + 20 + 10 + 30 + 10 = 80

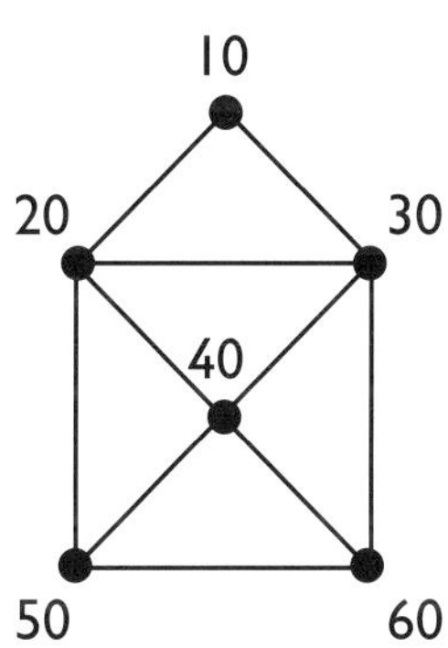

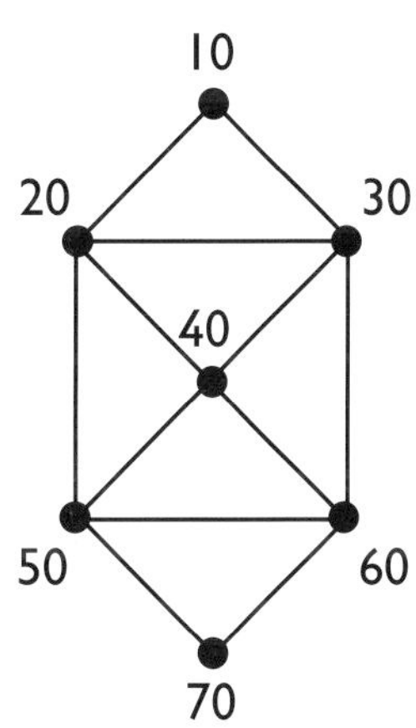

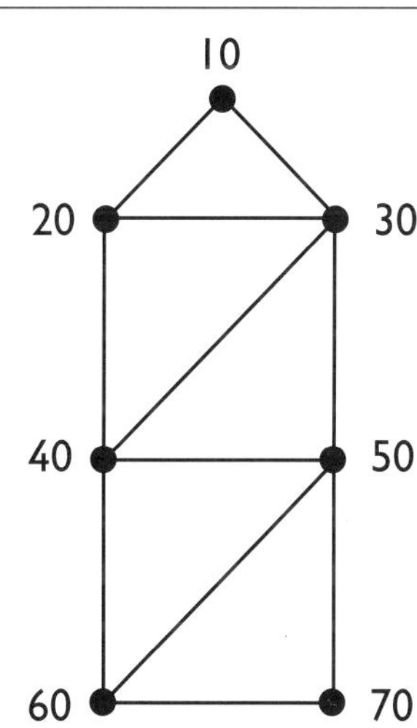

UNIT 19

River crossings

Use the methods shown to measure the widths of some imaginary rivers.
Record your methods and results.

Teaching objectives
- measuring and using angles
- solving practical problems
- explaining results

Resources
- PCM 19
- protractors
- measuring tapes and rulers
- chair, book, pencil, paper

Formative assessment
Can the children estimate and measure angles accurately?

Getting started

Give the children a copy of PCM 19 and give them a practical demonstration of how to set up this activity. Explain that the techniques rely upon the creation of a right-angled triangle and accurate measurement of distances and angles.

Key teaching point: Small inaccuracies in the measurement of an angle can be magnified to give large errors in length.

Independent task

Tell the children to investigate the problem by setting themselves a series of different rivers to measure. They should try Method 1 first. Tell them to record their actual findings and to compare these with the correct measurements. Ask them to explain how any inaccurate results were produced, and to suggest ways to improve their accuracy.

Developing the problem

- Invite children to show how they have recorded their work.
  Ask children to perform different roles in a practical demonstration of each of the methods.
- Show the children how to convert lengths on the scale drawings into actual distances using the *1 cm: 1 m* scale, for example:

  To convert 1·6 cm using this scale we multiply 1·6 by 100, which is 160 cm.
- Their next task is to work with a partner to use these methods to work out the width of the classroom.

FOLLOW-UP

- Explain how these methods could be adapted to work out the height of a building.
- Make a drawing of a triangle using the *1 cm: 1 m* scale. Challenge a partner to make a full size drawing of the triangle using chalk.

Drawing together

Invite children to show their methods of recording and explain any problems they encountered and any techniques they have learned that have helped them improve their accuracy.
Show the children how to adapt the methods to measure the height of a tree. For example:

- stand in a position at which the top of the tree is at an angle of 45 degrees to the ground
- measure the distance between your position and the tree
- add that distance to the height of your eyes above the floor to get an approximate height.

River crossings

Name ....

You need: a protractor, measuring tape or ruler, chair, book, pencil, paper

Use the methods shown to measure the widths of some imaginary rivers.

Record your methods and results.

Place two objects several metres apart, directly opposite each other on either side of an imaginary river.

Your task is to measure the distance between the objects without stepping in the river.

Method 1

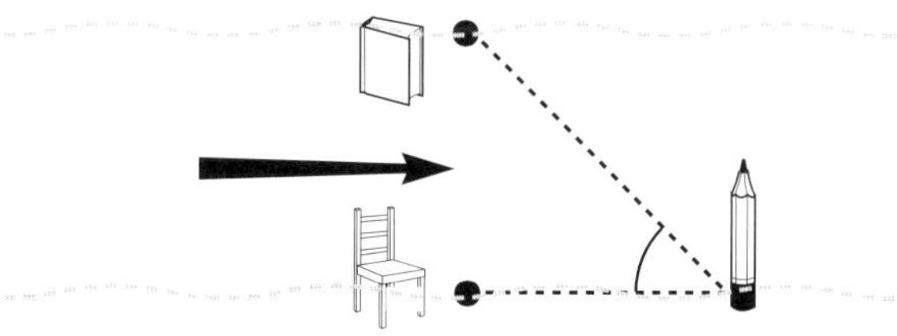

Walk in a straight line from the chair until you are at an angle of 45 degrees from the book. Mark the spot with a pencil.

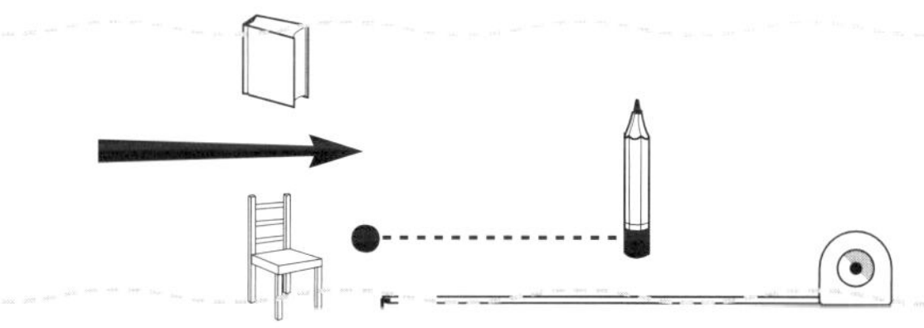

Measure the distance between the chair and the pencil.
This distance should be equal to the distance between the book and the chair.

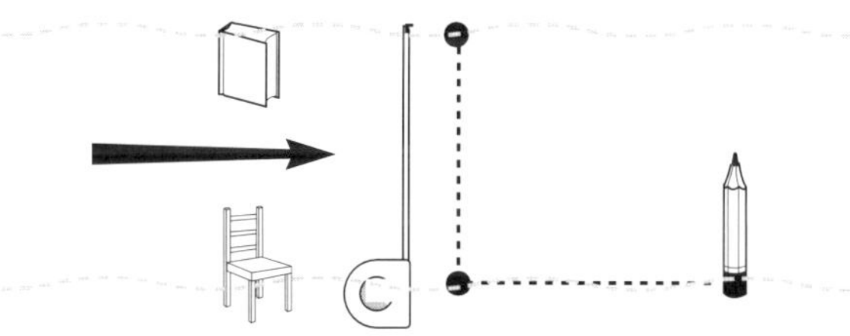

Check to see how accurate you were.

Method 2

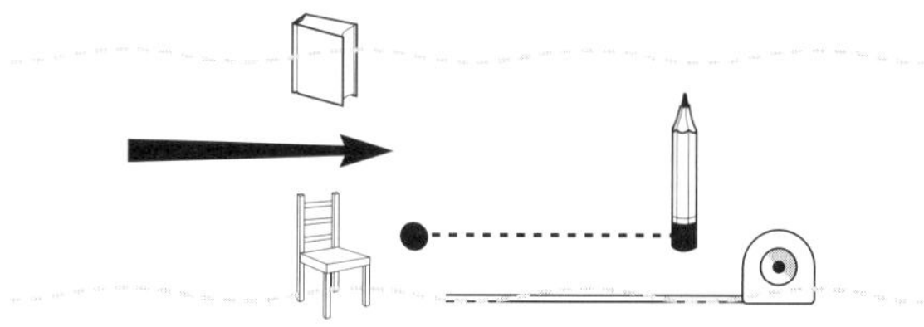

Measure a straight line to a point 10 metres from the chair and mark the spot with a pencil.

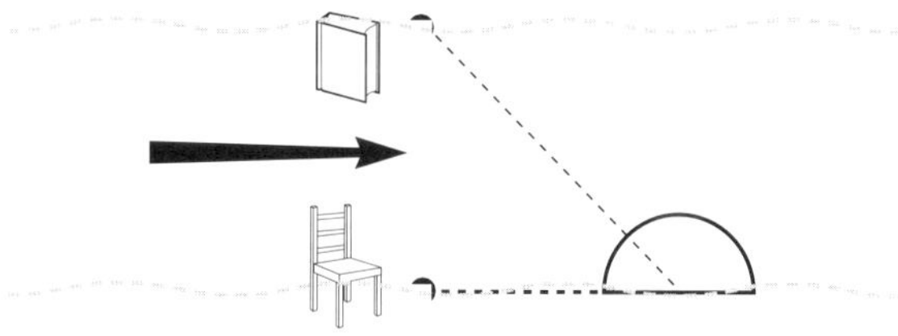

Place a protractor on this spot and look along it to work out the angle to the book.

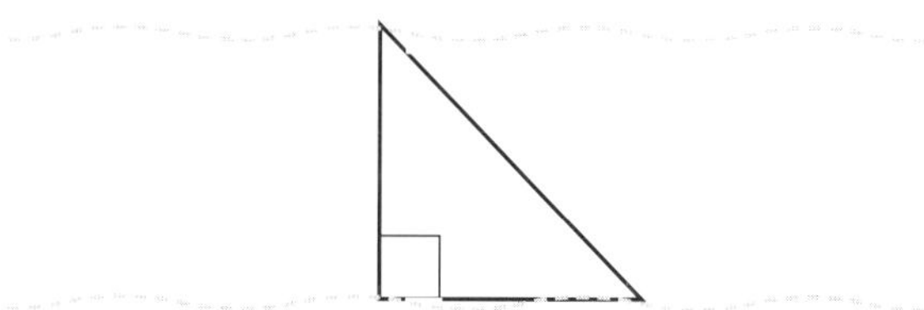

Draw a scale drawing of the right-angled triangle made by lines joining the chair, book and pencil using the scale 1 cm = 1 m.
Measure the distance between the chair and the book on the drawing and convert this into metres.
Check to see how accurate you were.

UNIT 20

Wholesome wholesale fruit & veg

Jessica buys three boxes of each type of fruit and vegetable to sell on her market stall.
She always buys the cheapest.
Work out which boxes she should buy.

Teaching objectives
- converting pounds into metric equivalents
- using all four operations to solve problems
- making decisions

Resources
- PCM 20
- paper
- calculators (optional)

Formative assessment
Can the children compare weights given in imperial and metric units?

Getting started

Give the children a copy of PCM 20 and explain the problem. Tell the children to complete the ready-reckoner equivalence poster. Ask them to explain how they would use the poster to find some equivalent weights, for example *10 kg, 20 lb, 7 kg, 7 lb*, and so on.
Show the children that the fractions used on the equivalence chart on the PCM give an approximate answer; $0{\cdot}45\ kg \times 2{\cdot}2\ lb = 0{\cdot}99\ kg$.

Key teaching point: Equivalence charts can be used to give approximate answers to conversion problems.

Independent task

Tell the children to work out which boxes Jessica should buy. Tell them to record all of the calculations used in their solution.

Developing the problem

- Invite children to explain how they solved some of the problems. Invite children to explain different methods used to calculate the same problem and to suggest how calculations could be checked.
- Show the children how to compare prices by converting all of the weights into the same unit (for example kilograms) and working out the price per kilogram;

Enosis Onions	*cost*	*£1.05 for 15 kg*
		£1.05 ÷ 15 = 7p per kilogram
Bunnion's Onions	*cost*	*£1.20 for 33 lb*
		33 lb ÷ 2·2 = 15 kg
		£1.20 ÷ 15 = 8p per kilogram

- Their next task is to work out how much money Jessica spent.

FOLLOW-UP

- Work out how much profit Jessica would make if she sold everything she bought for 7p per kilogram more than she paid for it.
- Draw a line graph that could be used to convert pounds into kilograms.

Drawing together

Give the children a calculator and ask them to follow the calculations used by children as they explain how they decided on which boxes to buy. Some may have encountered recurring decimals, and been unsure of how to round.
Invite children to demonstrate how some of the problems can be calculated using written methods.
Show the children that the fractions used in the equivalence chart only gives approximate answers which can be rounded, for example:
$48{\cdot}4\,lb \div 2{\cdot}2\,lb = 22\,kg$
$48{\cdot}4\,lb \times 0{\cdot}45\,kg = 21{\cdot}78\,kg$

Wholesome wholesale fruit & veg

Name ....

PCM 20

You need: reference books and magazines, paper for display

Jessica buys 3 boxes of each type of fruit and vegetable to sell on her market stall.

She always buys the cheapest.

Work out which boxes she should buy.

Ready-reckoner

pounds to kilograms		kilograms to pounds	
1 pound (lb)	= 0·45 kg	1 kilogram (kg)	= 2·2 lb
2 lb	=	2 kg	=
3 lb	=	3 kg	=
4 lb	=	4 kg	=
5 lb	=	5 kg	=

UNIT 21

Bridget's bridges

Bridget builds bridges.
Find the sections she'll need to build the bridges shown on her plans.

Teaching objectives
- using pencil and paper procedures to 2 decimal places
- devising procedures
- looking for patterns

Resources
- PCM 21
- paper

Formative assessment
Can the children add and subtract numbers to two decimal places?

Getting started

Give the children a copy of PCM 21 and explain the problem. Ask them to work out the length of the bridge shown on the poster. Tell them to work out the length of a bridge made from two of section A and three of section B, four of section B, and so on.

Key teaching point: Digits should be aligned in their correct columns when adding and subtracting using written methods.

Independent task

Tell the children to work out how to build each bridge. Tell them to present their work clearly so that it can be easily checked for errors. Tell them to record any methods used to make this problem more manageable.

Developing the problem

- Tell the children to swap their work with a partner and ask them to consider if the organization of the work makes it easy to check for errors. Invite children to explain any methods used that made the problem more manageable.
- Show the children how to simplify the problem by subtracting two of section A from the total lengths required, for example:
  Silvery Stream = 23·90 m − 16·38 m = 7·52 m.
  Section E = 7·52 m so the bridge will be built from two of section A and one of section E.
- Show them how to draw up a table of multiples of each length that can be used to help calculate the lengths, for example:

Section	×*1*	×*2*	×*3*	×*4*	×*5...*
A	–	*16·38*	–	–	–
B	*5·21*	*10·42*	*15·63*	*20·84*	*26·05*
C	*2·91*	*5·82*	...		

- Their next task is to find the length of a bridge made from two of each section.

FOLLOW-UP

- Find the sections needed to build a bridge across your playground.
- Find the widths of some real bridges and find which sections could be used to build bridges of the same length.

Drawing together

Invite children to explain their solutions to some of the problems. Display the solutions and ask children to check them, for example:

Squelchers Swamp = *94 m*
2 × section A = *16·38 m*
8 × section E = *60·16 m*
6 × section C = *17·46 m*
94·00 m

Bridget's bridges

Name ....

PCM 21

You need: paper

Bridget builds bridges.

Find the sections she'll need to build the bridges shown on her plans.

Bridge Building Basics

All bridges must have section A at each end and nowhere else.
Other sections fit in the middle.

A = 8·19 m B = 5·21 m C = 2·91 m D = 3·64 m E = 7·52 m F = 2·40 m

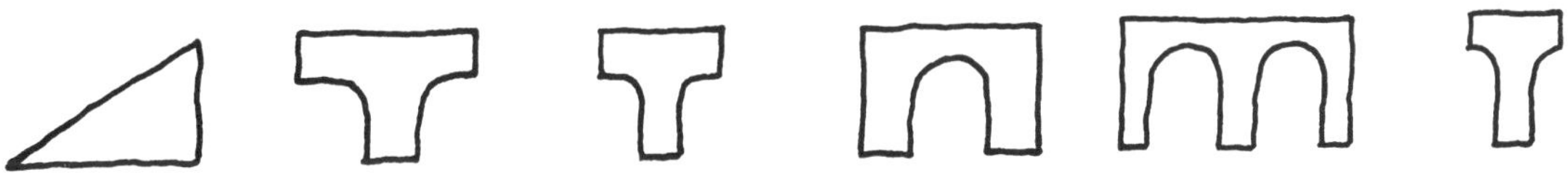

Here's an example

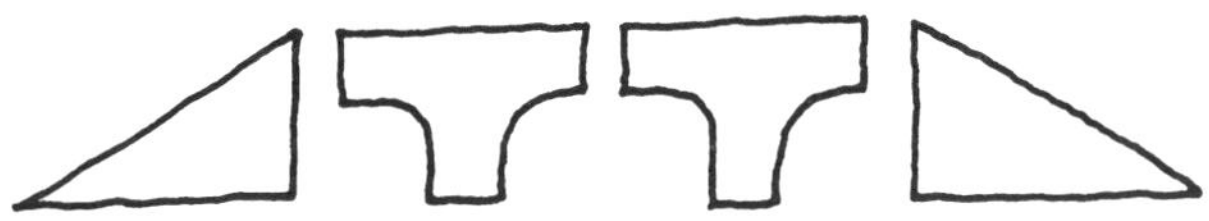

Section A 8·19 m Section B 5·21 m Section B 5·21 m Section A 8·19 m

Length of bridge = A + B + B + A = ______ m

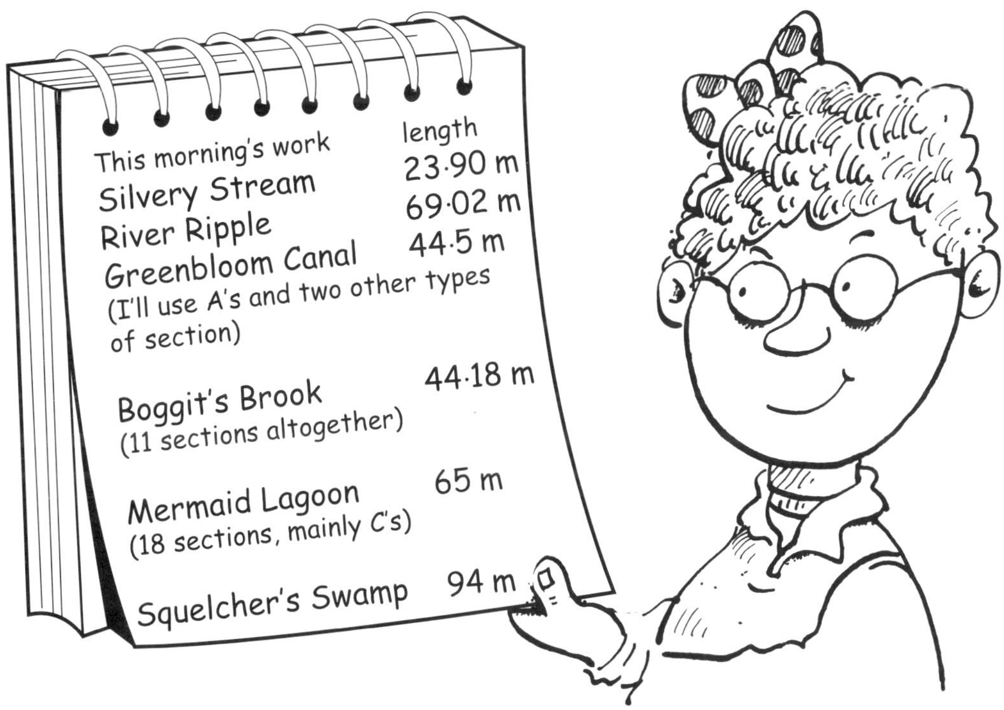

UNIT 22

The Secret Service telephone exchange

Secret Service agents phone each other using a secret code.
Use the instructions to work out how the following spies can be called.

Teaching objectives
- using all four operations to solve problems
- using trial and improvement methods
- explaining methods

Resources
- PCM 22
- calculators
- paper

Formative assessment
Can the children use brackets to dictate the order of multi-step operations?

Getting started

Give the children a copy of PCM 22 and explain the problem. Remind them how brackets are used to show the order in which operations should be completed, and that this can affect the final answer, for example:

$5 \times 5 - 5 = 20$ *or* 0 $\quad (5 \times 5) - 5 = 20 \quad 5 \times (5 - 5) = 0$

Ask the children to work out the example given in the instructions on the PCM and to find other totals that can be made by re-positioning the brackets.

Key teaching point: Brackets can be used to communicate and clarify the order in which calculations should be tackled.

Independent task

Tell the children to investigate the problem. Tell them to record how each telephone number can be made using the keys on the telephone. Ask them to make notes about any methods they found helpful in solving these problems.

Developing the problem

- Invite children to give the numbers and operations used in their solutions to some of the numbers and challenge the class to find the correct order of the calculation. Ask them to show the order using brackets.
- Show the children how to predict the types of operations used in the calculation by the size of the final total, for example *21141* is likely to have been made using multiplication whilst *4*, *16* and -3 are likely to have used subtraction or division.
- Show the children how to draw up multiplication and addition grids to be used as a reference in a trial and improvement approach, for example:

	×2	×3	×5	×7	×9	×13	×15	×25	×27	×29	×33
2	4	6	10	14	...						
3	6	9	...								

- Ask children to explain any methods used in solving the problems.
- Their next task is to find other totals that can be made by re-positioning the brackets in their solutions.

FOLLOW-UP

- Make up some more secret telephone numbers and challenge a partner to show how they were calculated.
- Use the telephone to see if it is possible to make numbers ending in *7*, *07* or *007*.

Drawing together

Invite children to explain their solutions and explain their methods.
Show them how to use divisibility tests to investigate some of the numbers, for example *21141* where the digits add up to 9, so we can divide by 9 to see if 9 might have been used in the calculation.
Similarly, *1225* ends in the digit 5, so 5 may have been used in the calculation.

The Secret Service telephone exchange

Name ....

PCM 22

You need: a calculator, paper

Secret Service agents phone each other using a secret code.

Use the instructions to work out how the following spies can be called.

UNIT 23

Neighbours

The children looked at a 1–100 grid.
Use their clues to work out what their mystery numbers could be.

Teaching objectives
- explaining methods and reasoning
- planning strategies
- looking for alternative solutions

Resources
- PCM 23
- 1–100 grid
- paper

Formative assessment
Can the children use 'multiples' tests to identify numbers?

Getting started

Give the children a copy of PCM 23 and explain the problem. Ask the children to underline any examples of mathematical vocabulary used in the clues. Invite children to explain the meanings. Ask the children to solve the first of the problems.

Key teaching point: Applying 'multiples' tests helps to simplify problems involving multiplication and division, for example, numbers ending in 5 are multiples of 5.

Independent task

Tell the children to investigate the rest of the mystery numbers. Tell them to record their methods and to include any information they used as a reference, for example, 'multiples' tests, lists of prime numbers, and so on. Tell the children to watch out for examples where more than one answer is possible.

Developing the problem

- Invite children to explain their solutions to some of the problems. Ask for examples of alternative methods or answers. Invite the children to explain any reference lists used in their working.
- Show the children how to mark the prime numbers up to 40 on the grid using Eratosthenes' sieve:
  Cross off 1. Start from 2 (but don't cross it off) and cross off every second number up to 40. Start from 3 (but don't cross it off) and cross off every third number, and so on. The numbers left are the prime numbers.
- Show them how highlighting these on the grid helps to focus the search, for example a ***number directly below a column of two prime numbers could be 33, 27 or 39.***

~~1~~	2	3	~~4~~	5	~~6~~	7	~~8~~	~~9~~	~~10~~
11	~~12~~	13	~~14~~	~~15~~	~~16~~	17	~~18~~	19	~~20~~
~~21~~	~~22~~	23	~~24~~	~~25~~	~~26~~	~~27~~	~~28~~	29	~~30~~
31	~~32~~	~~33~~	~~34~~	~~35~~	~~36~~	~~37~~	~~38~~	~~39~~	~~40~~

- Their next task is to write sets of clues for mystery numbers and then challenge a partner to find them.

FOLLOW-UP

- Write a set of clues to identify a set of numbers using clues which tell you what the numbers are not, for example: *These 2 consecutive numbers are not prime numbers and are not > 10.*
- Write a list of 'multiples' tests.

Drawing together

Invite children to explain their solutions to the problems.
Ask the children to add suggestions to a list of 'multiples' tests that can be displayed, for example: *Numbers are multiples of 3 if the sum of their digits is a multiple of 3. Numbers are multiples of 5 if the last digit is 0 or 5, and so on.*
Ask the children to find some mystery numbers, for example:
My number is next to a prime number and is a multiple of 4 and 7. (28)
My number is a multiple of 11 and touches a prime number at each corner. (22)
Invite children to set their own clues.

Neighbours

Name ....

You need: paper

The children looked at a 1–100 grid.

Use their clues to work out what their mystery numbers could be.

1	2	3	4	5	6	7	8	9	10
11	12	13	14	15	16	17	18	19	20
21	22	23	24	25	26	27	28	29	30
31	32	33	34	35	36	37	38	39	40
41	42	43	44	45	46	47	48	49	50
51	52	53	54	55	56	57	58	59	60
61	62	63	64	65	66	67	68	69	70
71	72	73	74	75	76	77	78	79	80
81	82	83	84	85	86	87	88	89	90
91	92	93	94	95	96	97	98	99	100

UNIT 24

Paper quadrilaterals

Teaching objectives
- using formulas to describe number sequences
- making and testing statements
- recognizing patterns and relationships

Resources
- PCM 24
- cm-squared paper

Formative assessment
Can the children use a formula to complete a series of calculations?

Jenny uses a 45° angle to draw a series of quadrilaterals.
Each shape is 2 cm wide.
She has calculated a formula to find the perimeter of each shape.
Find a formula to calculate the area of each shape and complete the table.

Getting started

Give the children a copy of PCM 24 and explain how the series of quadrilaterals have been drawn. Look at the formula used by Jenny to work out the perimeter of each shape. Tell the children to work out the perimeter of each shape using the formula and to check their answers on the diagram.

Key teaching point: The letters used in a formula describe a value in an abbreviated form, for example, *A = area, P = perimeter,* and so on.

Independent task

Tell the children to investigate the problem. Tell them to describe any patterns they notice in the answers and to keep a record of all of the formulas they attempt.

Developing the problem

- Display a large copy of the table and invite children to fill in the missing values for area and perimeter. Ask children to describe any patterns that they noticed in the table. Their next task is to investigate the area and perimeter of a series of quadrilaterals with a width of 1 cm drawn in a similar way.
- Show the children how spotting patterns allows you to check your answers, for example:

Q	*Area*	
1	*2 cm²*	
		+4 cm²
2	*6 cm²*	
		+4 cm²
3	*10 cm²*	

FOLLOW-UP

- Investigate formulas that can be used to calculate the area and perimeter of a series of quadrilaterals with a width of 3 cm drawn using the 45° line.
- Find formulas to calculate the area and perimeter of a sequence of squares.

Drawing together

Invite children to explain their formulas for calculating the area of each shape, for example: *Area = (Quadrilateral number × 4) subtract 2.* Test the formulas by working through some examples, for example:

$(Q \times 4) - 2 \quad = \quad Area$
$(1 \times 4) - 2 \quad = \quad 2\,cm^2$ *correct*
$(2 \times 4) - 2 \quad = \quad 6\,cm^2$ *correct and so on.*

Ask the children to use formulas to calculate the area and perimeter of quadrilaterals from the same series: *Q = 40, Q = 17, Q = 120, Q = 1000,* and so on.

Paper quadrilaterals

Name ....

You need: cm-squared paper

Jenny uses a 45° angle to draw a series of quadrilaterals.

Each shape is 2 cm wide.

She has calculated a formula to find the perimeter of each shape.

Find a formula to calculate the area of each shape and complete the table.

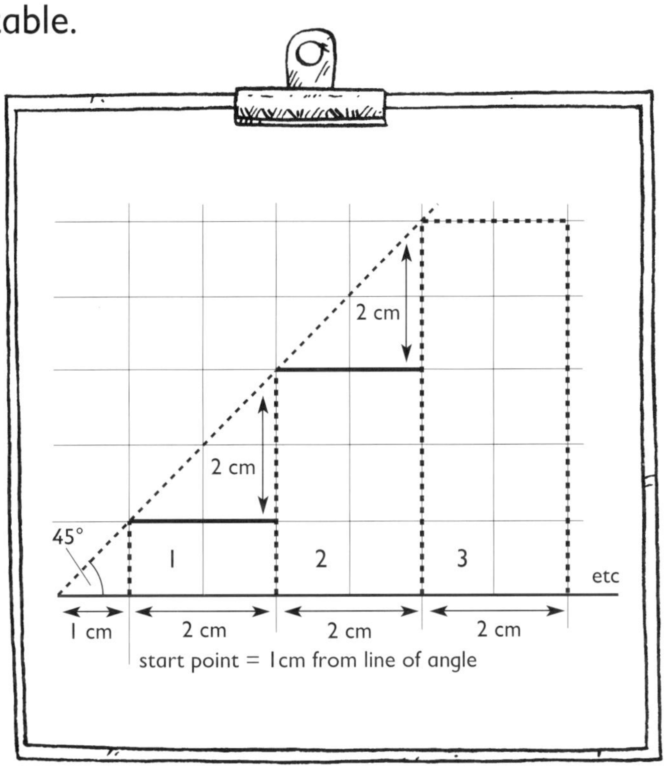

(Q x 4) + 2 = Perimeter in cm

(1 x 4) + 2 = 6

Perimeter = 6 cm

Quadrilateral number (Q)	Perimeter (P)	Area (A)
1	6 cm	
2		
3		
4		
5		
6		
7		
8		
9		
12		
33		
50		
100		

UNIT 25

Esti-mates

Teaching objectives
- making and explaining estimates of large numbers and quantities
- justifying answers
- creating new problems

Resources
- PCM 25
- paper

Formative assessment
Can the children make accurate estimates?

These children have set their partners a target number.
The challenge is to make three estimates that have answers close to that number.
Each estimate has to be justified.

Getting started

Give the children a copy of PCM 25 and explain the activity. Ask the children to look at the suggestions on the PCM and decide which are close to their target by finding approximate answers.

Key teaching point: Estimates can be used to check that answers to calculations are sensible and are also used where answers do not need to be precisely accurate.

Independent task

Tell the children to investigate the problem. Tell them to find at least three different estimates for each target and to show how each estimation can be justified. Ask the children to record some of the suggestions that they did not include after they proved to be too inaccurate when they tried to justify them.

Developing the problem

- Invite children to explain their solutions to some of the problems. Ask the children to justify their estimates using calculations and approximations. Ask the children to explain how they rounded numbers and decided upon the degree of accuracy required.
- Show the children how to justify an estimate, for example:
  I estimated that 4000 was the sum of the age in years of a class of 350 Year 6 children. I justified my answer using the calculation 350 × 11 = 3850.
- Ask the children to explain why this answer is only an approximation of the sum of their ages.

Is my estimate accurate enough? Is an estimate that was 150 too low more accurate when the target was 4000 or when it was 400 000? Why?

- Their next task is to set target numbers for a partner to estimate.

FOLLOW-UP

- Set yourself some decimal number targets to estimate.
- Estimate some measurement targets, for example the number of seconds taken to read 500 words, the total weight of 21 children identical to yourself, and so on.

Drawing together

Invite children to read out their estimates and challenge the class to find the target number they were estimating, for example:
The number of eggs in 700 half dozen boxes.(4000 = approximately 700 × 6)
The number of fingers on 1300 people. (10 000 = approximately 1300 × 8), and so on.

Esti-mates

Name ....

You need: paper

These children have set their partners a target number.

The challenge is to make three estimates that have answers close to that number.

Each estimate has to be justified.

UNIT 26

Quentin's quotient T-shirts

Teaching objectives
- working with fractions and decimals when dividing
- breaking down a problem
- looking for a range of solutions

Resources
- PCM 26
- paper

Formative assessment
Can the children interpret mixed numbers including fractions or decimals?

Quotient T-shirts are made by arranging the numbers in the box in the calculations on the T-shirts.
Show how the quotients for the T-shirts on the order form can be made.

Getting started

Give the children a copy of PCM 26 and explain the problem. Show the children how the numbers were arranged on the first T-shirt to give the answer $17\frac{1}{2}$. Ask them to explain how this quotient could be made using another arrangement of numbers on the T-shirt. Ask them to work out how the quotients on the other T-shirts were made.

Key teaching point: A good understanding of equivalent decimals and fractions is important when tackling division problems.

Independent task

Tell the children to investigate the other T-shirt quotients. Tell them to record how each quotient was made and to look for examples where it is possible to make the answer in more than one way. Ask them to write a few sentences explaining how answers can be checked.

Developing the problem

- Invite children to explain their answers to some of the problems. Ask them to explain how they approximated and calculated the division problem; how they checked and how they recorded their work.
- Show them how to find solutions to the problems using inverse operations and an understanding of equivalent fractions, for example:
  16·25 = $16\frac{1}{4}$. $\frac{1}{4}$ can be made by dividing 1 by 4.
  So the answer could be $(16 \times 4) + 1 \div 4$
  $16\frac{1}{4} \times 4 = 16 \times 4 = 64 + \frac{1}{4} \times 4 = 1 = 65$
  So $65 \div 4 = 16{\cdot}25$.
- Their next task is to find all of the quotients that can be made by dividing numbers greater than 70 by 2.

FOLLOW-UP

- Make up a series of calculations with missing numbers like the ones on the PCM. Challenge a partner to find the missing numbers.
- Find all of the quotients than can be made by dividing the numbers 24, 25 and 26. Arrange these numbers in order of size.

Drawing together

Invite children to give their solutions to some of the problems and look for alternative solutions. Ask them to suggest methods of making sure that a quotient ends in $\frac{1}{3}$ when dividing 3 (for example *any multiple of 3 + 1, divided by 3*).

How could you make sure that a number divided by 4 ended in ·25?
How could you make sure a number divided by 3 ended in ·666666?

Quentin's quotient T-shirts

Name ....

PCM 26

You need: paper

Quotient T-shirts are made by arranging the numbers in the box in the calculations on the T-shirts.

Show how the quotients for the T-shirts on the order form can be made.

100 90 80 70 60 50 40 30
20 10 6 5 4 3 2

order form

Order your T-shirts here

Name	Quotient Required
L. Owe	21·2
B. Kwyet	$9\frac{1}{3}$
Lee Nintower	16·25
Y. Knott	18·75
R. Yewshore	Any quotient ending in ·5
E. Biyeck	Any quotient ending in $\frac{1}{4}$
T. Fortew	Any number ending in $\frac{3}{5}$

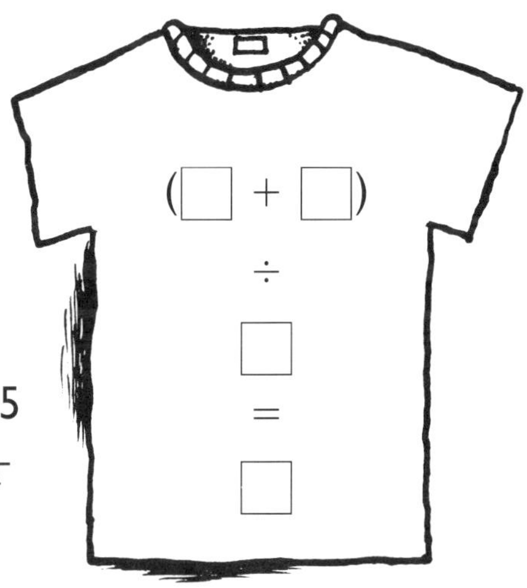

UNIT 27

Camp chef

Teaching objectives
- using multiplication and division
- collecting, organizing and recording information
- communicating clearly

Resources
- PCM 27
- information about food prices, for example, till receipts
- paper

Formative assessment
Can the children collect and use information effectively?

Your class are going camping and you have been chosen to do the cooking.
Draw up menus for each meal and work out what food supplies you will need to take with you.

Getting started

Give the children a copy of PCM 27 and explain the problem. Complete the information about the numbers of children and adults who will be taking part in the trip. Ask them to estimate the amount of bread and milk that will be required each day and to calculate the total cost of these items. Give the children some information about the cost of different food items, for example, till receipts.

Key teaching point: Multi-step problems need to be carefully recorded so that work can be checked and errors can be easily spotted.

Independent task

Tell the children to investigate the problem. Suggest that they simplify the problem by offering only one or two choices at each meal. You can ask different children or groups of children to work out menus for different days.

Developing the problem

- Invite children to show their work and explain how they have calculated some of their totals. Show the children examples of work that is clearly organized.
- Show the children how to set out their work in a tabular form:

Food item	*Price each*	*No. per plate*	*People on trip*	*Total cost*
Sausages	*12p*	*2*	*31*	*£7.44*
Eggs	*6p*	*1*	*31*	*£1.86*
Bacon	...			

- Ask the children how it is possible to find the cost of 1 egg or 1 sausage. Ask them if this sort of table could be used with items such as tins of beans or bottles of orange juice.
- Their next task is to calculate the cost of the trip for each child taking part.

FOLLOW-UP

- Calculate the cost of a fish-and-chip dinner and a visit to the swimming pool for the whole school.
- Calculate the cost of feeding yourself for 1 week. Show how you reached your answer.

Drawing together

Make a display of the work and invite children to explain how they reached some of their answers. Ask children to suggest methods for checking answers.
Ask for examples of problems where estimations and rounding of answers was required.
How could you work out the number of tins of peas/boxes of cornflakes/bottles of tomato sauce that would be needed?

Camp chef

Name ....

PCM 27

You need: paper

Your class are going camping and you have been chosen to do the cooking.

Draw up menus for each meal and work out what food supplies you will need to take with you.

Notes for the chef

Number of children ______

Number of adults ______

Arrive at Camp Quagmire 4 p.m. Monday

Leave for home 1 p.m. Friday

Meals needed

	Mon	Tues	Wed	Thurs	Fri
breakfast	✗	✓	✓	✓	✓
lunch	✗	✓	✓	✓	✓
evening meal	✓	✓	✓	✓	✗

Camp Quagmire supplies cooking equipment and basic supplies like salt and cooking oil free of charge.

Fresh bread (77p per loaf) and milk (34p per litre) can be supplied by neighbouring Manor Farm.

Dear Chef,

Please let me know the cost of the food A.S.A.P so I can add it to the £1300 it's costing for the campsite hire and transport. We need to share the total cost by the number of children so we know how much to charge each of them for the trip.

UNIT 28

Painting

Use the Comput-a-Quote form to work out the cost of painting your classroom.

Teaching objectives
- solving word problems involving measures
- converting imperial to metric units
- selecting materials to complete a task

Resources
- PCM 28
- rulers or tape-measures (imperial and metric)
- paper

Formative assessment
Can the children measure and record accurately?

Getting started

Give the children a copy of PCM 10 and explain the problem. Ask the children to work with a partner to complete a list of all of the measurements that will need to be made. Explain that they should approximate each measurement. Tell the children that a yard (3 feet) is just less than a metre (91·44 cm); a metre is 3 feet 3 inches (1·093 yards). Explain that they need to decide whether to approximate using decimals or feet and inches to represent yards. Tell them, if necessary, that there are 12 inches to a foot. Demonstrate with a ruler.

Key teaching point: Children need to be able to approximate measurements with some accuracy.

Independent task

Tell the children to work out the cost of painting their classroom. Ask them to keep a record of each of the measurements used in calculating their final quote.

Developing the problem

- Make a list of the final totals calculated by the children. Invite children to explain how they worked out different parts of the problem.

How did you work out the amount of skirting board paint required?
How did you convert yards into metric units?

- Show the children how to convert yards into metres and *vice versa* with greater accuracy:

  1 yard ≈ 0·9144 m so 20 yards ≈ 20 × 0·9144 = 18·28 m
  1 metre ≈ 1·093 yards so 10 metres ≈ 10 × 1·093 = 10·93 yards

- Their next task is to work out the area of walls and ceiling in square yards.
- Ask the children whether they think it would be easier for a decorator to work in yards, feet and inches, or in metres.

Why might some decorators still use imperial measures?

FOLLOW-UP

- Use the Comput-a-Quote form to work out the cost of painting a room in your home.
- Use the Comput-a-Quote form to work out the cost of painting your school hall.

Drawing together

Invite children to show their work. Ask them to explain where they found it appropriate to round measurements up or down and when approximate answers were acceptable, and when decimals were inappropriate for imperial measures. Invite children to approximate different lengths and ask them to explain any methods used. Explain that it might help to use multiples of your own height or to imagine multiples of metre-rulers or other objects of known length.

Painting

Name .... **PCM 28**

You need: : rulers or tape-measures (imperial and metric), paper

Use the Comput-a-Quote form to work out the cost of painting your classroom.

Record your work clearly.

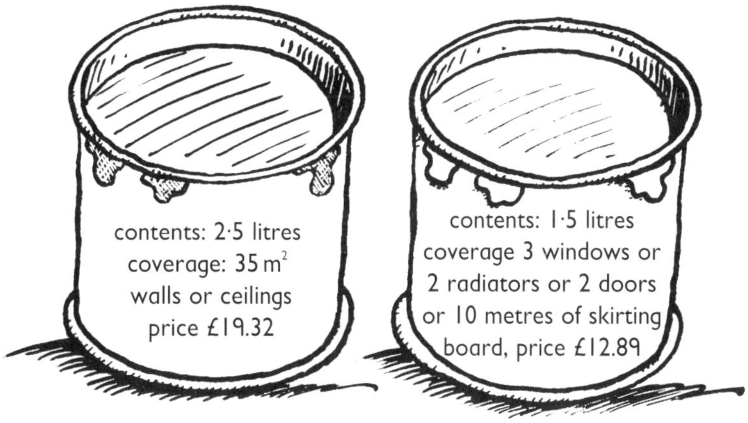

Dear Sir or Madam,
Thank you for your request for a quotation for painting your classroom in prawn pink and custard yellow.
Sloshons Ltd invite you to use our easy-to-use Comput-a-Quote form to work out your own quotation.

Comput-a-Quote

To work out a quote for painting your room:

1. Work out the labour costs

labour costs	£70 per day	________
preparation	1 day	________
walls and ceilings	2 days	________
	Sub-total	£________

2. Add these costs

radiators	£16.00 each	________
doors	£14.75 each	________
windows	£7.99 each	________
skirting board	£14.99 per 20 yards	________
	Sub-total	£________

3. Add cost of paint

Please note: All surfaces will be given 2 coats of paint.

walls and ceiling	£19.32 × _____ = £_____	________
doors and windows	£12.89 × _____ = £_____	________
and so on		
	Sub-total	£________
	Total of 1, 2 and 3	£________
4. Add 17·5% VAT	VAT	£________
5. Add all of the totals	Final total	£________

UNIT 29

Lunchingonline.co.uk

The creators of Lunchingonline.co.uk receive 15% of the profit made by their internet site. Use the tables to work out each person's monthly pay.

Teaching objectives
- solving problems involving percentages
- obtaining information from tables
- solving multi-step problems

Resources
- PCM 29
- paper

Formative assessment
Can the children organize their work and solve the problem in stages?

Getting started

Give the children a copy of PCM 29 and ask them to read the problem and discuss it with a partner. Tell them to draw a rough plan showing the stages needed to solve the problem. After a few minutes invite children to explain their plans. Invite children to explain how 10% of different amounts of money can be worked out using mental methods.

Key teaching point: 15% can be calculated mentally as 10% + half of 10%.

Independent task

Tell the children to work out each person's monthly pay, keeping a clear record of each stage of the calculations. Help the children to include a diagram in their working, showing the stages used to solve the problem.

Developing the problem

- Invite children to help complete a large copy of the table showing the total income and 15% profit.
- Show the children how to calculate 15% using different methods, for example:
  10% + 5% (half of 10%) = 15%
  3 × 10% = 30% shared by 2 = 15%
- Show the children that the three shares add up to 15 and that one part of the share can be worked out by dividing the profit total by 15. This figure can be multiplied to give the correct number of shares, for example:
  Profit for January = £189.15 ÷ 15 = £12.61
  Shares = £12.61 × 8 + £12.61 × 4 + £12.61 × 3
- Their next task is to work out each person's share if the profits were divided equally.

FOLLOW-UP

- Work out the monthly amount paid to each person if the creators received 75% of the profit.
- Work out the monthly amount paid to each person if the income for the next year increased by 50%.

Drawing together

Invite children to explain their approach to the problem and to show their methods of recording.
Explain how to divide a number by 15 using factors, for example:

300 ÷ 15 is the same as 300 ÷ 3 ÷ 5 $\quad 3\overline{)300}^{\,100} \quad 5\overline{)100}^{\,20}$

Explain that each person's share could have been worked out as multiples of 1% of the total profit, for example:
Income for January = £1261
1% of £1261 = £1261 ÷ 100 = £12.61
8 shares = £12.61 × 8 = £100.88

Lunchingonline.co.uk Name ....

PCM 29

You need: paper

The creators of Lunchingonline.co.uk receive 15% of the profit made by their internet site. Use the tables to work each person's monthly pay.

Profit-sharing table		
'Sandwich' Sal 8 parts of total 	'Juicey' Jim 4 parts of total 	'Chocbar' Chas 3 parts of total 

	Profit			
Month	Weekdays	Weekends	Total profit	15% of profit
Jan	£770	£491		
Feb	£893	£268		
Mar	£990	£367		
Apr	£1255	£121		
May	£212	£606		
June	£401	£700		
July	£906	£431		
Aug	£67	£19		
Sept	£580	£670		
Oct	£604	£604		
Nov	£990	£268		
Dec	£467	£764		

UNIT 30

Donna's disappearing digits and brackets

Teaching objectives
- using a calculator to solve problems involving brackets
- using trial and improvement methods
- creating new problems

Resources
- PCM 30
- calculators
- paper

Formative assessment
Can the children use a logical trial and improvement method to find solutions?

Donna has made up a series of problems with missing numbers and missing brackets.
Find the missing numbers and put the brackets in the correct place.
Find what other answers can be made in each problem by moving the brackets.

Getting started

Give the children a calculator and a copy of PCM 30 and explain the problem. Make sure that the children understand that in each problem only one number is used and that the number used will not be the same for each problem. Ask children to explain why brackets are used in calculations. Tell the children to investigate different answers that can be made from a series of calculations, for example:

$5 \times 5 + 5 \times 5$ $\quad$ $8 \times 8 - 8 + 8$ $\quad$ $9 + 9 \times 9 \div 9$

Key teaching point: Brackets are used to indicate the order in which a calculation is completed because different sequences of operations can produce different answers.

Independent task

Tell the children to investigate the problem. Tell them to record every calculation used in any trial and improvement approach. Tell them to record their alternative answers from moving brackets separately to the answers to Donna's problems.

Developing the problem

- Invite children to explain the number used in some of the problems and challenge children to work out where the brackets should be placed to give the correct answer.
- Show the children how to organize and record a trial and improvement approach, for example:

  Target $7{\cdot}29$ $\quad$ $3 \times 3 = 9$ *too high*
  $2 \times 2 = 4$ *too low so answer is between 2 and 3*
  $2{\cdot}5 \times 2{\cdot}5 = 6{\cdot}25$ *too low, and so on.*
- Show children how to use the memory function on the calculator.
- Their next task is to make up a series of five similar problems for a partner to solve.

FOLLOW-UP

- Write a set of instructions showing how to use the memory function on a calculator.
- Work out the order in which a calculator completes its operations and try to find out if all calculators use the same order.

Drawing together

Invite children to give their solutions to the problems. Look at records of trial and improvement methods used in finding solutions. Invite children to suggest other answers that can be made by changing the position of the brackets and ask children to check these using a calculator.
Compare the answers obtained using the memory function with those made when the calculations are entered in the same order as shown on the page. Ask the children to explain what the calculator is doing.

Donna's disappearing digits and brackets

Name ....

You need: a calculator, paper

Donna has made up a series of problems with missing numbers and missing brackets.

Find the missing numbers and put the brackets in the correct place.

Find what other answers can be made in each problem by moving the brackets.

Write the same number in each box for each problem.

8	×	8	+	8	= 72			
☐	×	☐	×	☐	= 729			
☐	×	☐	−	☐	= 380			
☐	×	☐	+	☐	×	☐	= 338	
☐	+	☐	×	☐	+	☐	= 2916	
☐	+	☐	×	☐	×	☐	= 5488	
☐	×	☐	+	☐	+	☐	= 1155	
☐	×	☐	÷	☐	= 17			
☐	×	☐	= 7·29					

Each shape stands for a number.

Find out the number of each shape.

✧ × □ = 1064 ○ + ✧ = 27

△ × ○ = 568 □ ÷ ○ = 7

✧ − ○ = 11

UNIT 31

Sports centre manager

Teaching objectives
- interpreting pie charts
- making statements based on findings
- justifying answers

Resources
- PCM 31
- paper

Formative assessment
Can the children make statements based on the information presented in pie charts?

Bianca is comparing the data on the children's clubs organized at the two sports centres she manages.
Use the data to suggest how each centre might provide a better service.

Getting started

Give the children a copy of PCM 31 and explain the problem. Ask them to write a series of questions and statements based on the data. After a few minutes invite children to challenge the class to answer their questions.

Key teaching point: Pie charts can be analysed using fractions to compare the sizes of segments to obtain approximate numbers.

Independent task

Tell the children to investigate the problem and to write a report suggesting the changes that should be made in each sports centre. Tell them to support their suggestions by referring to the data.

Developing the problem

- Draw a large copy of the pie charts and invite children to explain how they could calculate the approximate numbers of customers shown by each segment.
- Show the children how to start by using segments representing approximately a quarter or a third of the total and comparing other segments with these. Show them how to work out the approximate numbers of customers, for example: ***This segment represents a quarter of the total. A quarter of 360 = 360 ÷ 4 = 90.***
- Invite children to explain which clubs need to be re-scheduled and re-priced.
- Their next task is to work out the approximate amount of money taken by each club at the different sports centres.

FOLLOW-UP

- Your improvements lead to a 20% increase in attendance at each club. Work out the approximate amount of money that will be taken by each club.
- Your improvements lead to a 70% fall in attendance at each club. Work out the approximate amount of money that will be taken by each club.

Drawing together

Make a display of the finished work and invite children to explain their recommendations. Ask them to explain how they have used the data to support their findings.
Ask children to solve a series of questions based on fractions and percentages, for example:
What fraction/percentage is equal to 25%, $\frac{3}{4}$, 33%, $\frac{1}{5}$, $\frac{3}{5}$, 80%, $\frac{1}{100}$?
What is $\frac{1}{4}$ of 900, 10% of 570, $\frac{1}{3}$ of 315?

Sports centre manager

Name .... PCM 31

You need: paper

Bianca is comparing the data on the children's clubs organized at the two sports centres she manages.

Use the data to suggest how each centre might provide a better service.

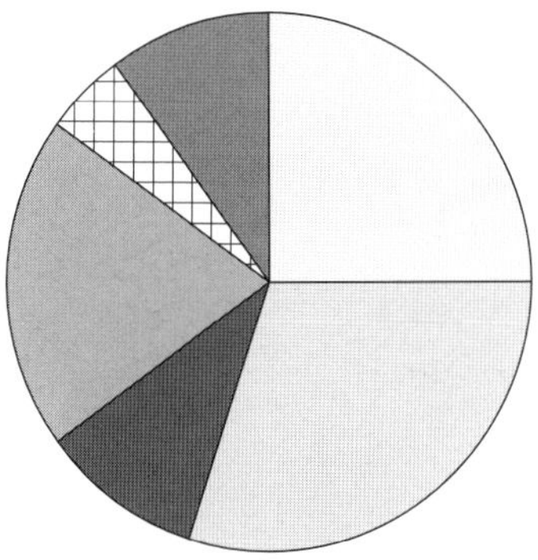

Happy Valley Sports Centre

- 25% swimming
- 30% nursery basketball
- 10% after school club
- 20% badminton
- 5% hockey
- 10% tennis

Total attendance 800

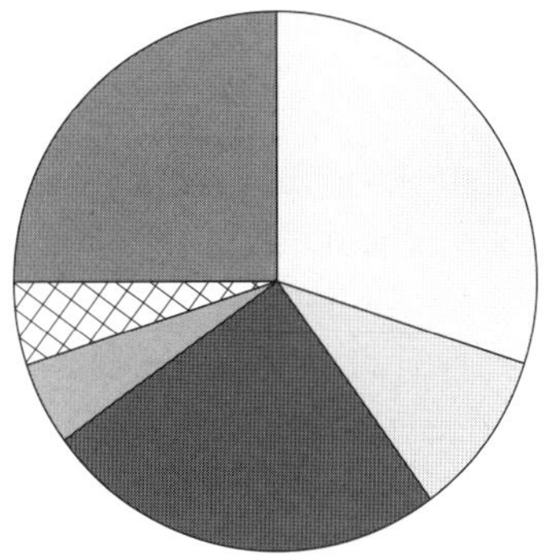

Pitts Lane Sports Centre

- 30% swimming
- 10% nursery basketball
- 25% after school club
- 5% badminton
- 5% hockey
- 25% tennis

Total attendance 360

Customer Satisfaction Survey Results

	H.V.S.C.	P.L.S.C.
Is the centre clean?	85% Yes	11% Yes
Are the staff helpful?	25% Yes	73% Yes
Are the prices too high?	29% Yes	80% Yes
Are the times suitable?	69% Yes	29% Yes
Other clubs you would like.		
Karate	15%	5%
Volleyball	67%	56%

	Times and Prices			
	H.V.S.C.		**P.L.S.C.**	
Swimming	3:30 – 5 p.m.	90p	3 – 4:30 p.m.	£7
Nursery basketball	10 – 11 p.m.	80p	9 – 10 p.m.	£3.20
After school club	2:15 – 4 p.m.	£4	4 – 7 p.m.	£9
Badminton	3:45 – 6 p.m.	£8	3:45 – 6 p.m.	£8
Hockey	3:15 – 6 p.m.	90p	11 p.m – 1 a.m.	£12
Tennis	3:40 – 6:15 p.m.	80p	3:45 – 7 p.m.	80p

UNIT 32

Symmetrilectric shirt designs

Teaching objectives
- exploring pattterns in rotation and symmetry
- using coordinates
- giving accurate instructions

Resources
- PCM 32
- cm-squared paper
- tracing paper

Formative assessment
Can the children plot coordinates in all four quadrants?

The Symmetrilectric Shirt Design robots are used to print patterned shirts.
Robots are used to translate, rotate or reflect shapes drawn in any quadrant.
Robot programs express direction using points of the compass, and measure distance in centimetres.
Use the programs to draw the designs and invent programs to make your own patterns.

Getting started

Give the children a copy of PCM 32 and explain the problem. Draw a large copy of the labelled axes on cm-squared paper and invite children to mark a series of coordinates on this copy. Draw a square in one quadrant and invite children to give the coordinates of a reflection/rotation/translation of that shape.

Key teaching point: Accurate mathematical language is necessary when describing shapes.

Independent task

Tell the children to investigate the problem keeping accurate records of the designs produced. Tell them to design their own programs for the robots and to draw the designs produced.

Developing the problem

- Display a large copy of the axes and invite children to help plot one of the designs chosen from the PCM. Invite children to show their own versions of the designs.
- Show the children how to rotate a shape around a point using a pencil point placed on the coordinate and a copy of the shape drawn on a piece of tracing paper.
- Their next task is to write the program for a design that uses the compass directions north-east, north-west, south-east or south-west.

FOLLOW-UP

- Design a program for a pattern based on a triangle rotated repeatedly through 30° clockwise.
- Design a program for a pattern made using mirror lines placed diagonally between the x- and y-axes.

Drawing together

Make a display of the patterns. Hide the programs used to make each design beneath a folded slip of paper and challenge the children to work out how each design was made.
Invite children to challenge a partner to use their program to produce an accurate version of their design.

Symmetrilectric shirt designs

Name ----------------------------------

You need: cm squared paper, tracing paper

The Symmetrilectric Shirt Design robots are used to print patterned shirts.

Robots are used to translate, rotate or reflect shapes drawn in any quadrant.

Robot programs express direction using points of the compass, and measure distance in centimetres.

Use the programs to draw the designs and invent programs to make your own patterns.

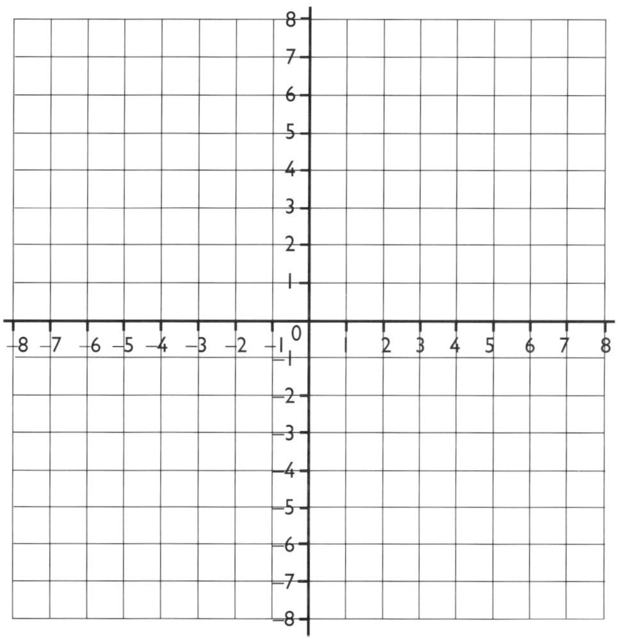

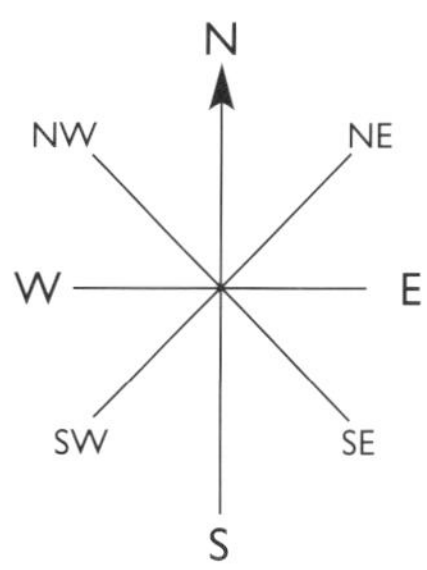

Design 1

Start at (–8, 0)

Repeat, until you reach the y-axis, the sequence made by drawing a line North 2, East 3, South 1, West 1

Reflect it in mirror lines on the x- and y-axes.

Design 2

Draw a hexagon with vertices at (0, 0), (−3, 0), (−6, 3), (−6, 6), (−3, 6), (0, 3)

Rotate it around (0, 0) 90° clockwise. Draw the rotated shape. Repeat.

Design 3

Draw a triangle with vertices at (0, −8), (−4, −6), (0, −5)

Translate it by moving each coordinate 1 square North and 1 square West. Draw. Repeat until you reach the x-axis.

Reflect it in a mirror line on the x-axis.

Design 4

Start at (−2, 6).

Repeat, until you reach the x-axis, the sequence made by drawing a line East 1, North 2, West 2, South 3.

Reflect it in mirror lines on the x- and y-axes.

UNIT 33

The race

A group of animals set out on a 300 kilometre race on 1st January 2000.
Use the information given to work out the order in which they finished.

Teaching objectives
- solving story problems involving measurement and time
- converting units from imperial to metric
- selecting appropriate methods

Resources
- PCM 33
- paper
- calculators

Formative assessment
Can the children convert imperial to metric units and *vice versa*?

Getting started

Give the children a copy of PCM 33 and explain the problem. Ask them what additional information they will require in order to complete the problem and ask them to suggest where they might find it. Tell the children to discuss the problem with a partner and to estimate what they think was the finishing order.

Key teaching point: Measurements expressed in different units should be converted into a common unit to make it easier to compare them.

Independent task

Tell the children to work out the finishing order. Tell them to record all of the calculations used to reach their final answer and to set out their work in a clear and organized way. Remind them that 5 miles is about 8 kilometres, and 1 yard is just shorter than a metre.

Developing the problem

- Invite children to give what they think was the finishing order and explain their solutions to different parts of the problem. Ask them to suggest ways of checking some of the answers.
- Show the children how they could convert kilometres into miles, for example:
  The tortoise walks 8 miles each day.
  5 miles $\approx$ 8 kilometres
  So 8 miles $\approx$ (8 $\times$ 8) $\div$ 5 miles $\approx$ 12·8 km.
  So we now need to work out how many lots of 12·8 km make 300 km.
  Ask children to suggest how this can be done, using a calculator as appropriate.
- Their next task is to give the approximate date and time of each finisher.

FOLLOW-UP

- Find out the average speeds of other animals and calculate the time it would take them to cover a distance of 300 kilometres.
- Calculate the average speed of each animal in kilometres per hour.

Drawing together

Make a display of the children's work. Compare the finishing order with the original predictions. Look for examples where rounding has led to differences in final answers.
Display these approximate equivalents;
8 km $\approx$ 5 miles
1 foot $\approx$ 30 cm
Challenge the children to convert a series of distances, for example: ***6 feet, 1 yard, 10 miles, 35 miles, 2·5 feet, 7$\frac{1}{2}$ miles, 32 kilometres, 12 kilometres, 1·2 metres, 3 metres, and so on.***

The race

Name ....

You need: a calculator, paper

A group of animals set out on a 300 kilometre race on 1st January 2000.

Use the information given to work out the order in which they finished.

UNIT 34

How now? Which cow?

Each village in Wallopshire chooses a new cow every year.
The villagers measure in pints and gallons but the information about the cows has been given in litres.
Decide which cow will give each village the amount of milk they need.

Teaching objectives
- converting pints and gallons to metric units
- selecting appropriate methods and operations
- checking results

Resources
- PCM 34
- calculators
- paper

Formative assessment
Can the children use an equivalence chart to convert units of measurement?

Getting started

Give the children a coloured pencil, a calculator and a copy of PCM 34. Explain the problem. Ask the children to work with a partner to highlight all of the information that is needed to answer the problem. Explain how to use the conversion chart, for example:
The number of pints equivalent to 100 litres is equal to 100 divided by 0·568 which is approximately 176.
Show them how to round the answers to give approximate answers and to check their calculations using a different method, for example:
176 pints ÷ 8 = 22 gallons. 22 × 4·546 litres = approximately 100 litres.

Key teaching point: Calculations using equivalence charts often produce answers which need to be rounded to give approximate equivalents.

Independent task

Tell the children to work out which cow is best suited to which village. Tell them to record all of the calculations used to decide which cow was chosen for each village and all methods used to check answers.

Developing the problem

- Invite children to explain their solution to some of the problems by mapping out the stages on a large piece of paper, for example:
  15 pints ⟶ change this to litres/day ⟶ find out how many litres/day each cow gives ⟶ match the closest to the village
- Tell children to use a calculator to follow some of the calculations used.
- Their next task is to work out which cow or combination of cows would produce enough milk to give each member of your school 1·5 litres per day.

FOLLOW-UP

- Find out how much milk would be produced in a year by a herd containing 10 of each type of cow.
- Use the chart to find the equivalent capacity of some household containers.

Drawing together

Invite children to explain how they decided which cow to choose for each village. Show the children how to tackle the problem by converting the amount of milk produced by the cows into pints and gallons, for example:
Bell 19 litres ÷ 0·568 = approximately 33 pints/day
33 pints per day × 7 = 231 pints per week
33 pints per day × 365 = 12 045 pints per year

How now? Which cow?

Name ....

You need: a calculator, paper

Each village in Wallopshire chooses a new cow every year.

The villagers measure in pints and gallons but the information about the cows has been given in litres.

Decide which cow will give each village the amount of milk they need.

UNIT 35

Getting classrooms on-line

Teaching objectives
- using all four operations to solve problems
- selecting appropriate materials and methods
- presenting results

Resources
- PCM 35
- equipment for measuring length
- paper

Formative assessment
Can the children solve calculations involving decimals?

The classrooms in your school are going to be connected to the office by train lines.
Model trains will be used to carry messages.
Work out which boxes of Traintrack will be needed to build train lines between your classroom and the office.

Getting started

Give the children a copy of PCM 35 and explain the problem. Ask children to suggest which measurements they'll need to make in order to solve this problem. ***At which point should the train line begin/end? What happens to the length of the line if it has to go around corners? What equipment should we use to measure the route?*** Ask the children to work out the change from £99.50 if you bought two of each type of box.

Key teaching point: Decimal points should line up when using standard written methods.

Independent task

Tell the children to investigate the problem. Tell them to keep a record of all measurements and calculations and to include a map explaining the route of the train line and the boxes of traintrack used to build it.

Developing the problem

- Invite children to explain how they measured the route of their train line and worked out the different boxes of track required.
- Show the children how to use a tape measure or piece of string to work out the lengths of flexible track needed to build the track around corners.
- Their next task is to calculate the cost of buying the traintrack needed to build their route and to work out if it is possible to build a cheaper route using the same materials.

FOLLOW-UP

- Design train lines to connect other classrooms in the school. Start by drawing a plan of the relevant parts of the school.
- Design a system of train lines to connect your rooms at home.

Drawing together

Make a display of the children's work and draw attention to examples of work that most clearly record the stages in which the problem was tackled.
Display examples of errors in calculations and ask the children to explain what mistakes have been made, for example:

$$\begin{array}{r} 0{\cdot}15 \\ +\ \ 0{\cdot}24 \\ \hline 0{\cdot}174 \end{array} \qquad \begin{array}{r} 40 \\ -\ 0{\cdot}24 \\ \hline 0{\cdot}16 \end{array} \qquad \begin{array}{r} 40{\cdot}00 \\ -\ \ \ 0{\cdot}24 \\ \hline 40{\cdot}24 \end{array}$$

Invite children to give examples of methods used to check calculations.

Getting classrooms on-line

Name ....

You need: a ruler or measuring tape, paper

The classrooms in your school are going to be connected to the office by train lines.

Model trains will be used to carry messages.

Work out which boxes of train track will be needed to build train lines between your classroom and the office.

Draw a plan of the route of the train lines from your classroom to the office. Mark the measurements on it.

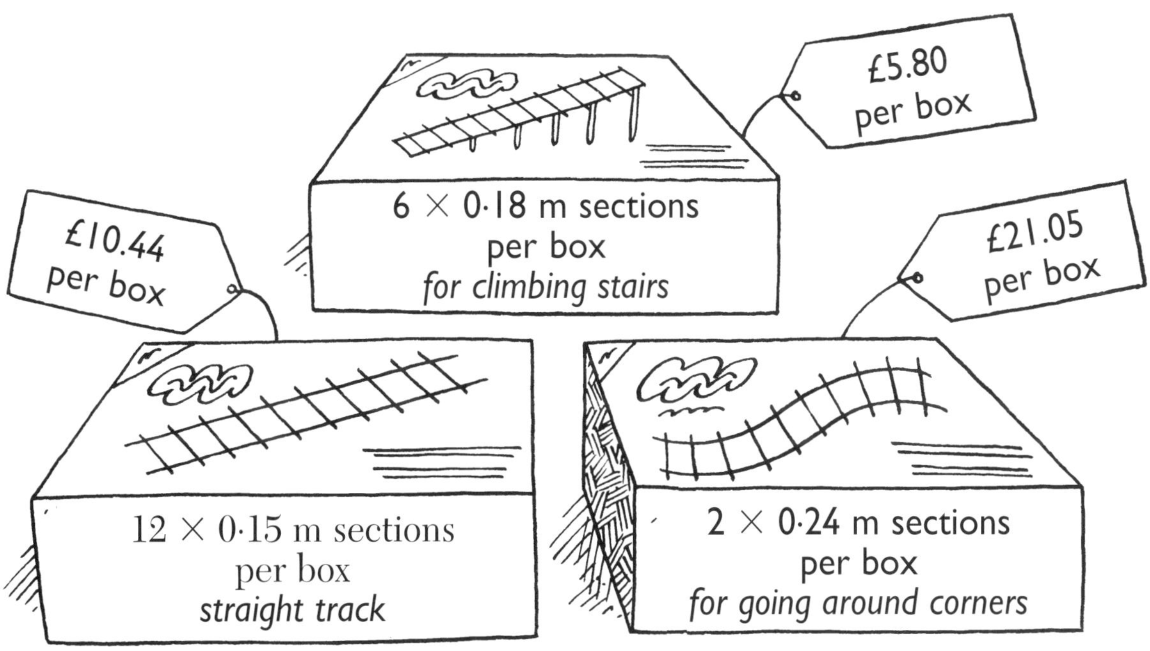

UNIT 36

Baby Bighead's building bricks

Teaching objectives
- using prime factors
- working systematically
- looking for connections

Resources
- PCM 36
- paper

Formative assessment
Can the children find the prime factors of numbers up to 120?

Baby Bighead says he can make 80 of the numbers between 10 and 120 with his building bricks.
His friend thinks it's impossible.
Show which of the babies is correct.

Getting started

Give the children a copy of PCM 36 and explain the problem. Ask the children to predict how many numbers can be made by multiplying just three bricks. Ask them to test their predictions.

Key teaching point: Every number is either a prime number or can be produced as a product of prime numbers.

Independent task

Tell the children to investigate the problem keeping a record of how each number was made. Tell them to record all of the numbers that could not be made.

Developing the problem

- Invite children to explain how they have organized and recorded their work. Look at examples that show a systematic approach.
- Show the children how to organize their search by keeping all but one of the numbers constant until all possible combinations have been found, for example:
  2 × 3 × 2 × 2 = 24
  2 × 3 × 2 × 3 = 36
  2 × 3 × 2 × 5 = 60 and so on.
- Their next task is to find which additional numbers they could make with an extra 2, 3 and × brick.

FOLLOW-UP

- List the numbers which could no longer be made without the 2 bricks.
- Which numbers could be made if the 2 and 3 bricks were replaced by a set of number 4 bricks?

Drawing together

Invite the children to help to complete a list of the numbers which cannot be made using the bricks. Ask them to check to see if this list is correct and to explain anything they notice about these results.
Ask the children to explain any techniques they developed that helped them complete the task.
Invite children to play a game in which they take it in turns to make two of the numbers from the problem of the week using mental arithmetic. The questions can be set and checked by other members in the class, for example:
Make 44.
Explain which bricks you would use to make 80.

Baby Bighead's building bricks

Name ....

You need: paper

Baby Bighead says he can make eighty of the numbers between 10 and 120 with his building bricks.

His friend thinks it's impossible.

Show which of the babies is correct.

1	2	3	4	5	6	7	8	9	10
11	12	13	14	15	16	17	18	19	20
21	22	23	24	25	26	27	28	29	~~30~~
31	32	33	34	35	36	37	38	39	40
41	42	43	44	45	46	47	48	49	50
51	52	53	54	55	56	57	58	59	60
61	62	63	64	65	66	67	68	69	70
71	72	73	74	75	76	77	78	79	80
81	82	83	84	85	86	87	88	89	90
91	92	93	94	95	96	97	98	99	100

1 Number snooker

The following properties are worth discussing with children. The first two are general properties of number; the next two are specific to this problem. Encouraging the children to make use of these properties instead of using trial and error should lead them to adopt an analytical approach.

Multiplying then dividing by the same number leaves the number you started with; for example,
0·5 × 100 ÷ 100 = 0·5.
The order of the operations does not matter; for example, 1·402 × 1000 ÷ 10 × 2 will give the same answer as 1·402 ÷ 10 × 2 × 1000.
Multiplication will increase the value of the ball, whilst division will decrease it.
With the exception of the use of the '× 2 cushion' and the 'triple score pocket', the actual significant digits of the numbered balls will remains unchanged, only the place values change.

Some ways to make the target numbers:

an odd number	175 × 2 ÷ 10 = 35
a number ≥ 1 million	4000 × 1000 = 4 000 000
a number ≤ 0·004	0·2 × 2 ÷ 1000 = 0·0004
6 million	60 × 10 ×10 × 1000
27 000	9 × 1000 × 3 (triple score pocket)
1·402	701 × 2 ÷ 1000
60	60 × 10 ÷ 10
8000	4 000 × 2
12	60 × 2 ÷ 10
0·06	60 ÷ 100 ÷ 10
3500	175 × 2 × 10
120	60 × 2
200 000	10 × 2 × 1000 × 10
150	0·5 × 10 × 10 × 3 (triple score pocket)
540	9 × 2 × 10 × 3 (triple score pocket) (a tricky shot!)

2 Stone Age calculators

The key here is a good knowledge of multiplication bonds (up to 9 × 9) and understanding the use of these in factorising. Encourage children to recognize numbers that are exact products of single digit multiplication (for example 28, 56 and 81). When faced with numbers that are not products of single digit multiplication, a good strategy is to divide the number by a single digit. For example, dividing 288 by 4 gives 72, so 288 can be entered as 4 × 8 × 9. Trickier are prime numbers; for these an alternative method is needed, as explained in *Drawing together*.

The multiples of 10 can be made as follows:
10 = 2 × 5
20 = 4 × 5
30 = 6 × 5
40 = 8 × 5
50 = 5 × 2 × 5
60 = 2 × 6 × 5
70 = 2 × 7 × 5
80 = 2 × 8 × 5
90 = 2 × 9 × 5
100 = 2 × 5 × 2 × 5

The homework problems (example answers)
28 × 14 = 7 × 4 × 7 × 2 = 392
15 × 24 = 5 × 3 × 6 × 4 = 360
18 × 12 = 6 × 3 × 6 × 2 = 216
100 × 56 = 2 × 5 × 2 × 5 × 9 × 7 = 5600
72 × 21 = 9 × 8 × 7 × 3 = 1512
810 ÷ 18 = 9 × 9 × 2 × 5 ÷ 9 ÷ 2 = 45
288 ÷ 12 = 4 × 8 × 9 ÷ 6 ÷ 2 = 24
56 × 90 = 8 × 7 × 9 × 2 × 5 = 5040
49 × 42 = 7 × 7 × 7 × 6 = 2058
21 × 23 = (20 × 20) + (20 × 3) + (1 × 20) + (1 × 3) = (5 × 4 × 5 × 4) + (4 × 5 × 3) + (4 × 5) + (1 × 3) = 383
240 ÷ 15 = 6 × 4 × 2 × 5 ÷ 3 ÷ 5 = 16
81 × 36 = 9 × 9 ÷ 9 ÷ 4 = 2916
17 × 13 = (10 × 10) + (10 × 3) + (7 × 10) + (7 × 3) = (5 × 2 × 5 × 2) + (5 × 2 × 3) + (7 × 5 × 2) + (7 × 3) = 221
504 ÷ 4 = 63; 7 × 9 = 63; so 4 × 9 × 7 = 504
21 × 2 = 42; 7 × 6 = 42; so 7 × 6 ÷ 2 = 21
64 × 25 = 8 × 8 × 5 × 5 = 1600
18 × 2 × 2 = 9 × 2 × 2 × 2 = 72; so 72 ÷ 2 ÷ 2 = 18

3 Coconut shy

The best approach to this problem is to draw up a table showing the result produced by each ball knocking down each coconut. Able children could use a spreadsheet to do this, or you can reproduce it for children to work from.

	Coconut					
Ball	147	3405	7 942	7·2	106	8951
3	441	10 215	23 826	21·6	318	26 853
4	588	13 620	31 768	28·8	424	35 804
5	735	17 025	39 710	36·0	530	44 755
6	882	20 430	47 652	43·2	636	53 706
7	1029	23 835	55 594	50·4	742	62 657
8	1176	27 240	63 536	57·6	848	71 608
9	1323	30 645	71 478	64·8	954	80 559
10	1470	34 050	79 420	72·0	1060	89 510

Solutions

1323	(9 × 147) + two misses
17 025	(5 × 3405) + two misses
57·6	(8 × 7·2) + two misses
390	(3 × 106) + (10 × 7·2) + one miss
1438·2	(3 × 147) + (6 × 7·2) + (9 × 106)
90 774	(3 × 3405) + (9 × 8951) + one miss
116 253	(7 × 147) + (4 × 8951) + (10 × 7942)

4 Can you keep a secret?

As well as the formal methods for converting between improper fractions and mixed numbers and for finding sets of equivalent fractions, it is often possible to find the letters by exploiting mental strategies and by approximating. Some examples:
$\frac{13}{6}$ – since double 6 is 12, the solution must be slightly more than 2, giving *t*.
$\frac{36}{144}$ – half of 144 is 72 and half of 72 is 36, so $\frac{1}{4}$ is the equivalent fraction, giving *a*.

5 Wear & Wave Ltd

It is useful to consider the different percentages required in relation to 10%. This allows much of the calculation to be done mentally with paper and pencil needed for recording the composite parts. It is useful to realize the following:

To find 15% – find 10% then add on half the result again.
To find 30% – find 10% then triple the result.
To find 35% – find 10%, triple it, then add half of 10% again.

Other percentages that can be found easily by recognizing fraction equivalents are 1% (divide by 100), 2% (double 1%), 25% (divide by 4) and 50% (divide by 2).
Number of items likely to be sold on each match day, and the money likely to be spent (to the nearest pound):

	17th Nov	26th Dec	13th April	4th May
Scarf	6750 (£4719)	8000 (£55 920)	1800 (£12 582)	49 500 (£346 005)
Hat	4500 (£15 525)	10 000 (£34 500)	5 400 (£18 630)	36 000 (£124 200)
Flag	4500 (£11 250)	8800 (£22 000)	4 320 (£10 800)	27 000 (£67 500)
Shirt	20 250 (£261 023)	14 000 (£180 460)	720 (£9281)	72 000 (£928 080)
Hands	450 (£446)	4000 (£3960)	720 (£713)	18 000 (£178 200)
Profits (to nearest £)	£3159	£3883	£1123	£17 550

6 All the fun of the fair

The children should see quite quickly that the suggested charges are somewhat unrealistic. Next, they need to consider the following points. Answers will depend on the choices they make.

1 Likely attendance: the children could use last year's figure or work with an average of the last four years.
2 What is a reasonable charge for each attraction?
3 What opportunity should be given for people to win the games of chance? Is it better to have a few large prizes or a greater number of smaller ones?
4 What size portions should be sold at the food and drinks stalls?

7 Goal scorers

The goal scoring record for each player can be considered in terms of the three types of average.
To find the mode: identify the tallest bar on the graph.
To find the median: consider the number of games played and count along to the halfway point. For example, Chambers has played 20 games so the median is between his 10th and 11th score, i.e. 1 goal.
To find the mean: find the total number of goals scored and divide by the number of games played in. Chambers scored 1 goal 5 times, 2 goals 7 times and 4 goals once. That is, he scored 23 goals in 20 games, giving a mean of 1·15 goals per game.

Answers (means are given to two decimal places)

	Mode	Median	Mean
Chambers	0·2	1	1·15
Taylor	0	1	0·86
Howard	0	1	0·95
Walsom	0	0	1·06
Gibbs	0	0·5	1·07
Akinmoya	1	2	1·77
Clifford	0	1	1·38

8 Video-link homework conferencing

A good way to record the solutions pictorially is to mark points equidistant on a circle to show each computer then join each point to every other point. It is then straightforward to see how many cables are used.
For example, for 6 children linking up, the diagram would be:

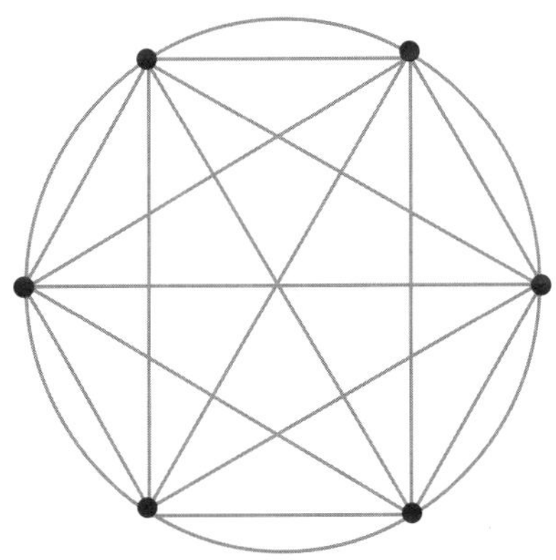

Table of results

Number of children	Number of cables	Price
2	1	£99.97
3	3	£299.91
4	6	£599.82
5	10	£999.70
6	15	£1499.55
7	21	£2099.37
8	28	£2799.16
9	36	£3598.92
10	45	£4498.65

Children should spot the pattern. For each child added to the network, the number of cables increases by one more than it did for the previous additional child. The children might recognize the results as being the triangular numbers.

Another way of explaining this is to think of the number of connections each child needs. For example, if there are 6 children, each child has to be connected to all 5 other children. That is $6 \times 5 = 30$ connections. In fact, though, this is twice the number of cables we need, since each cable makes two connections (A to B and B to A). Algebraically this can be expressed as $n \times (n - 1) \div 2$ or $n(n - 1) \div 2$.

9 Chimp on a tricycle

It is a good idea to have a child 'walk the pattern', or to use a floor robot to demonstrate the basic idea.

The completed patterns will look like this:

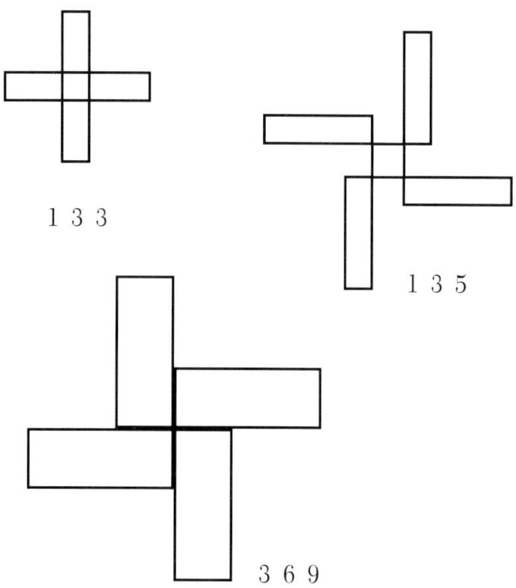

Distances travelled:

1 28 cm **2** 28 m **3** 36 km **4** 36 m **5** 72 m **6** 72 cm

10 Glenda's global restaurant

Children should be encouraged to use mental strategies to solve these problems. For example, to find the time to put on the chicken, we need to start with the serving time, 9:10 p.m. The chicken takes 85 minutes to cook, so we should put it on at 7:45 p.m., since, counting backwards and using the 'whole hours' as a bridge, $10 + 60 + 15 = 85$.

Answers

	Washington	London	Brussels	Athens	Tokyo	Canberra
Fish soup	12:28 a.m.	7:28 p.m.	6:28 p.m.	5:28 p.m.	10:28 a.m.	9:28 a.m.
Chicken	12:45 a.m.	7:45 p.m.	6:45 p.m.	5:45 p.m.	10:45 a.m.	9:45 a.m.
Chips	1:59 a.m.	8:59 p.m.	7:59 p.m.	6:59 p.m.	11:59 a.m.	10:59 a.m.
Carrots	1:48 a.m.	8:48 p.m.	7:48 p.m.	6:48 p.m.	11:48 a.m.	10:48 a.m.
Apple Pie	2:26 a.m.	9:26 p.m.	8:26 p.m.	7:26 p.m.	12:26 p.m.	10:26 a.m.
Custard	2:42 a.m.	9:42 p.m.	8:42 p.m.	7:42 p.m.	12:42 p.m.	10:42 a.m.

11 Aristotle the arithmetic aardvark

A good strategy here is to get children to make numbers in different ways that can then be used as 'building blocks' for the target numbers. For example, 1000 might be 10 000 − 9000, 9000 − 8000 and so on. 500 might be 300 + 200 or 400 + 80 + 20. Using these and other building blocks should help the children generate many different solutions for the target number 1570.

12 Squares and tables

Square	Total
1	4
2	12
3	20
4	28
5	36

Square	Total
6	44
7	52
8	60
9	68
10	76
30	236

Once the pattern of '+ 8' has been noticed the 30th square can be found by adding 160, i.e. 20×8, to 76 (the 10th square total). The pattern is generated by the formula, $8 \times n - 4$. The pattern for multiples of 3 will go up by 12 each time, 6, 18, 30, 42.... and, so is generated by $12 \times n - 6$.

13 Overdrawn at the bank

Some points to note:

1 To find the starting income add £845 to the bank statements of 1st March.

2 Information in the speech bubbles is critical to finding solutions.

3 The table of solutions can be reproduced with some cells blanked out (number of cells blanked out can be varied according to the ability of the children).

	Income	Clothes	House	Car	Holiday	Debt
Kevyn	£914	£3121	£35 195	£415	£760	£38 577
Davy	£3377	£675	£199 000	£13 000	£8456	£217 754
Wavy	£2765	£490	£213 000 £444 999	£17 656	£214	£673 594
Sharyn	£2351	£21	£174 250	£13 265	£678	£185 863

14 Cuddly toys

To get started with this problem, it is a good idea is to draw up a table showing the various possible single dart scores. This can then be used to look for combinations that give the target numbers as totals.

The table will look something like this:

single score	double	× 6	× 7
10	20	60	70
20	40	120	140
30	60	180	210
.... 200	400	1200	1400

When working out the multiples of 6 and 7, children should be encouraged to make connections to known number facts and mental methods. For example, they might find 70 × 6 by realizing that 7 × 6 = 42, and so 70 × 6 = 420. From this they should be able to move by doubling to 140 × 6 = 840.

15 Cargo ships

The children need to begin by completing the tables.

Document 1:	**Schedule**	
Ship	*Destination*	*Cargo when full in kilograms*
Ark	Hull	1 235 000
Art	Singapore	1 330 000
Artemis	Riga	1 140 000
Arch	New York	1 805 000
Aries	Lisbon	2 090 000
Archer	Naples	1 710 000

The remaining sand should be distributed as follows: 570 000 kg to Arch, 760 000 kg to Aries and 570 000 kg to Archer.

16 Congratulations: You've won a holiday!

Country	£375 buys	£1 buys
Jamaica	$23 625	$63
Japan	61 562·81¥	164·17¥
New Zealand	$1234.73	$3.29
Syria	£25 184	£67.16
United States	$562.50	$1.50

When comparing the costs of the same item in different countries it is useful to do an approximation first as this sometimes renders it unnecessary to do an accurate calculation. For example a CD in Japan costs 2000 yen which, at 164·17 yen to the pound is more than £10. In the United States the CD costs $13, which at $1.50 to the pound is less than £10. A calculator is usually appropriate for exact solutions.

17 Fractions in an 'L'

It is useful to begin by finding the decimal equivalent of each fraction. Since each fraction will be used 11, 9, 7, 5 or 3 times, it is also useful to work out these multiples of each fraction.

A reference table can be drawn up to show these:

	× 3	× 5	× 7	× 9	× 11
$\frac{3}{4}$	2·25	3·75	5·25	6·75	8·25
$\frac{1}{2}$	1·5	2·5	3·5	4·5	5·5
$\frac{1}{4}$	0·75	1·25	1·75	2·25	2·75
$\frac{1}{5}$	0·6	1	1·4	1·8	2·2
$\frac{1}{10}$	0·3	0·5	0·7	0·9	1·1

Trying different combinations should help find solutions. Each row is made of a different number of cards, and of a different fraction. Therefore, to find the total for any given grid, 6 multiples need to be added together, one from each row and one from each column. It is helpful to look at how the tenths digits add to give the desired total.

2·75 is made up of an 'L' of 11 quarters

15·1 is made from 3 fifths, 5 tenths, 7 quarters, 9 three-quarters and 11 halves.

12·7 is made from 3 tenths, 5 three-quarters, 7 fifths, 9 halves and 11 quarters.

18 The intersection question

A good strategy here is first to find a way of drawing each shape without lifting pencil from paper or retracing any steps. Then the numbers can be moved around to find the largest and smallest possible totals.
To make a large total, the larger numbers should be at the most visited junctions. To make a smaller total, the largest numbers should be at the least visited junctions.
One way to describe the routes is to list the numbers passed through:
Some examples (not necessarily the only solutions):
Drawing 1 30, 20, 10, 20, 30; largest possible: 120; smallest possible: 70.
Drawing 2 20, 10, 20, 10; largest possible: 60; smallest possible: 60.
Drawing 3 50, 40, 30, 20, 40, 60, 50, 20, 10, 30, 60; largest possible: 410; smallest possible: 360.
Drawing 4 50, 40, 30, 20, 40, 60, 50, 20, 10, 30, 60, 70, 50; largest possible: 600; smallest possible: 440.
Drawing 5 20, 10, 30, 20, 40, 30, 50, 40, 60, 70, 50, 60; largest possible: 550; smallest possible: 490.

19 River crossings

Method 1 This method makes use of the properties of a right-angled isosceles triangle. Setting the angle at the pencil to 45° means that the angle at the book will also be 45°. Since the two angles are the same, the three objects are the points of an isosceles triangle, where the distance between book and chair, and between pencil and chair, are equal.

Method 2 With this method it is important to be accurate to the nearest degree in measuring the angle as any error here will be amplified when 'scaling up' the lengths.

20 Wholesome wholesale fruit and veg

Where the price is quoted per kilogram, divide the cost by the number of kilograms. Where the price is quoted per pound, first divide the number of pounds by 2·2, then divide the price by the number of kg to convert to pence per kg. The costs for each type of fruit and vegetable can then be compared directly. The results will differ slightly if the children multiply by 0·45 to find the price in pounds.

Costs per kilogram:	
Grannies Apples	35p
Gramp's Apples	40p
Hewman Beans	44p
Ayleeyen Beans	50p
Enosis Onions	7p
Bunnion's Onions	8p
Won Potatoes	9p
Tew Potatoes	8p
Care Pears	54p
Bear Pears	55p
Yewsay Tomatoes	32p
Isay Tomatoes	29p

The total weight of produce bought and sold should be calculated in kilograms (125 kg). Three boxes of each produce will therefore weigh 375 kg (3 × 125 kg). The profit will therefore be £26.25 (375 × £0.07).

21 Bridget's bridges

The following table shows the length (in metres) of up to 10 of each piece.

Section	× 1	× 2	× 3	× 4	× 5
A		16·38			
B	5·21	10·42	15·63	20·84	26·05
C	2·91	5·82	8·73	11·64	14·55
D	3·64	7·28	10·92	14·56	18·20
E	7·52	15·04	22·56	30·08	37·60
F	2·40	4·80	7·20	9·60	12·00

Section	× 6	× 7	× 8	× 9	× 10
A					
B	31·26	36·47	41·68	46·89	52·10
C	17·46	20·37	23·28	26·19	29·10
D	21·84	25·48	29·12	32·76	36·40
E	45·12	52·64	60·16	67·68	75·20
F	14·40	16·80	19·20	21·60	24·00

Two 'section A's' are needed for each bridge, so we can straight away subtract 16·38 from any of the required lengths before considering the other pieces.
To help children towards a solution you can copy the table for them to use. It would also be useful to have an OHT (if possible) or a large copy to use during class discussion.

Answers:
Silvery Stream: 2 × Section A + 1 × Section E
River Ripple: 2 × Section A + 7 Section E
Greenbloom Canal: 2 × Section A + 4 × Section B + 2 × Section D
Boggit's Brook: 2 × Section A + 5 × Section D + 4 × Section F
Mermaid Lagoon: 2 × Section A + 10 × Section C + 5 × Section F + 1 × Section E
Squelcher's Swamp: 2 × Section A + 6 × Section C + 8 × Section E

22 The Secret Service telephone exchange

You need to be careful to make sure the children are using brackets correctly. You might like to have number and operation cards available for children to move around to create number sentences. You can also blu-tack these to the board during the plenary to demonstrate what happens when the position of the brackets is moved.

Examples of ways in which the spies can be phoned:
9801 = 33 × 3 × 33 × 3
176 = (3 + 5) × (7 + 15)
21141 = 9 × 29 × 9 × 9
–3 = 27 + 33 – (7 × 9)
448 = (13 + 15) × (7 + 9)
2116 = (13 + 33) × (13 + 33)
16 = (33 ÷ 3) + 3 + 2
4 = (29 + 3) ÷ (3 + 5)
1225 = (7 × 7) × (5 × 5)

23 Neighbours

24 Paper quadrilaterals

To help children explore the pattern it is a good idea for them to copy the sequence of quadrilaterals onto centimetre-squared paper. You will probably need to remind the children not to confuse the units of area and of length.

Area in square centimetres = Q × 4 − 2

Quadrilateral number	Perimeter	Area
1	6 cm	2 cm^2
2	10 cm	6 cm^2
3	14 cm	10 cm^2
4	18 cm	14 cm^2
5	22 cm	18 cm^2
6	26 cm	22 cm^2
7	30 cm	26 cm^2
8	34 cm	30 cm^2
9	38 cm	34 cm^2
12	50 cm	46 cm^2
33	134 cm	130 cm^2
50	202 cm	198 cm^2
100	402 cm	398 cm^2

25 Esti-mates

Approximate answers for the first example:
Minutes in 66 hours = 60 × 66 = 3960
Pennies in 150 metres = 50 × 15 = 750 (If a penny is 2 cm wide, there are 50 in a metre.)
People on 18 buses = 18 × 80 = 1440

Clearly 4000 is a good estimate of the number of minutes in 66 hours; for the buses and coins it is little more than a guess.

These initial answers make useful benchmarks for tackling the rest of the problem. Although the children will be using multiplication in their justifications, in order to make these 'backwards estimates', it is useful to find approximations to division questions. For example, they might ask themselves how many times 24 will go into 10 000 (the 2nd target number) while working towards an estimate involving time.

26 Quentin's quotient T-shirts

It is useful here to consider the order of the operations; all the questions are in the form:

(□ + □) ÷ □ = □

But in each case there are different known and unknown numbers. The use of inverse operations helps solve most of these problems.
For example, on the third T-shirt, the two missing numbers must total 32, since dividing their sum by 5 must give 6·4. For L. Owe's T-shirt, 21·2 × 5 =106, so we need (100 + 6) ÷ 5.

The first four T-shirts:
$(30 + 40) \div 4 = 17\frac{1}{2}$
$(10 + 6) \div 3 = 5\frac{1}{3}$
$(30 + 2) \div 5 = 6.4$
$(100 + 90) \div 2 = 95$;

and the T-shirts ordered:

Name	Quotient Required	Calculation
L. Owe	21·2	(100 + 6) ÷ 5
B. Kwyet	$9\frac{1}{3}$	(50 + 6) ÷ 6
Lee Nintower	16·25	(60 + 5) ÷ 4
Y. Knott	18·75	(70 + 5) ÷ 4
R. Yewshore	Any quotient ending in ·5	for example: (20 + 30) ÷ 4
E. Biyeck	Any quotient ending in $\frac{1}{4}$	for example: (20 + 5) ÷ 4
T. Fortew	Any quotient ending in $\frac{3}{5}$	for example: (20 + 3) ÷ 5

27 Camp Chef

The solutions will vary according to the menus the children design and the cost of the food they work with.

28 Painting

When working out the surface areas scale drawings of the classroom would be a useful starting point. It is best to carry out all measurements in metres (since the prices are all quoted in metres). However, it is interesting to note that many decorators do still work in imperial units.

29 Lunchingonline.co.uk

You can help the children draw this diagram to show the stages of the calculation.

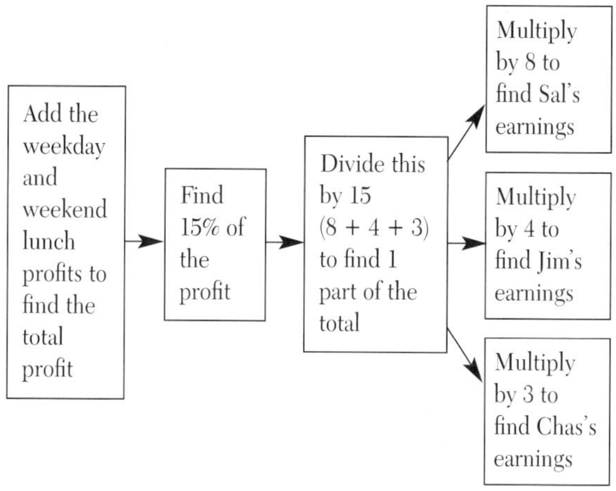

	Profit						
Month	Weekdays	Weekends	Total	15% of	'Sandwich'	'Juicey'	'Chocbar'
Jan	£770	£491	£1261	£189.15	£100.88	£50.44	£37.83
Feb	£893	£268	£1161	£174.15	£92.88	£46.44	£34.83
Mar	£990	£367	£1357	£203.55	£108.56	£54.28	£40.71
Apr	£1255	£121	£1376	£206.40	£110.08	£55.04	£41.28
May	£212	£606	£818	£122.70	£65.44	£32.72	£24.54
Jun	£401	£700	£1101	£165.15	£88.08	£44.04	£33.03
Jul	£906	£431	£1337	£200.55	£106.96	£53.48	£40.11
Aug	£67	£19	£86	£12.90	£6.88	£3.44	£2.58
Sep	£580	£670	£1250	£187.50	£100.00	£50.00	£37.50
Oct	£604	£604	£1208	£181.20	£96.64	£48.32	£36.24
Nov	£990	£268	£1258	£188.70	£100.64	£50.32	£37.74
Dec	£467	£764	£1231	£184.65	£98.48	£49.24	£36.93

30 Donna's disappearing digits and brackets

As with many problems of this type, where we start with the answer and work backwards, it is important to use inverse operations.

9 × 9 × 9 = 729
(20 × 20) − 20 = 380
13 × 13 + 13 × 13 = 338
(27 + 27) × (27 + 27) = 2916
(14 + 14) × 14 × 14 = 5488
33 × 33 + 33 + 33 = 1155
(17 × 17) ÷ 17 = 17
2·7 × 2·7 = 7·29

Shapes:

○ = 8 ◇ = 19 □ = 56 △ = 71

31 Sports centre manager

Children should use the equivalence of percentages and fractions to manipulate the data. They should also use mental strategies to derive less obvious percentages, finding 5% by halving 10% or 30% by multiplying 10% by 3.

When discussing improvements for the sports centres, make sure the children strike a balance between customer needs and profit.

	Happy Valley		Pitts Lane	
Club	Attendance	Money taken	Attendance	Money taken
Swimming	200	£180	108	£756
Basketball	240	£192	36	£115.20
After school club	80	£320	90	£810
Badminton	160	£1280	18	£144
Hockey	40	£36	18	£216
Tennis	80	£64	90	£72

32 Symmetrilectric shirt designs

Design 1

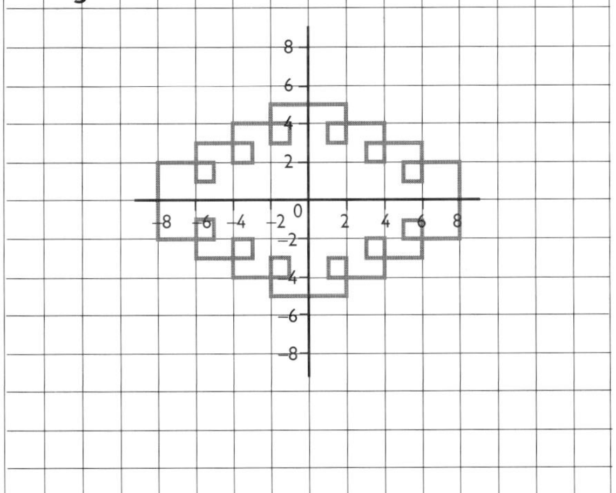

Design 2

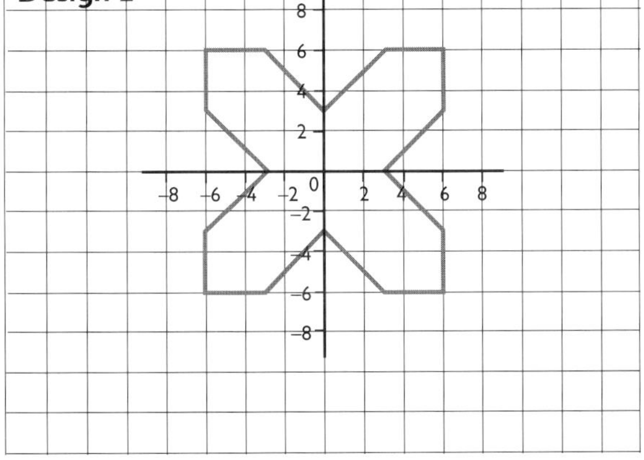

Design 3

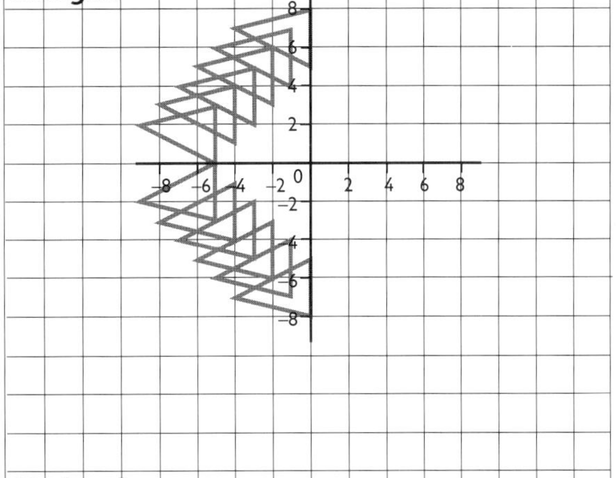

Design 4

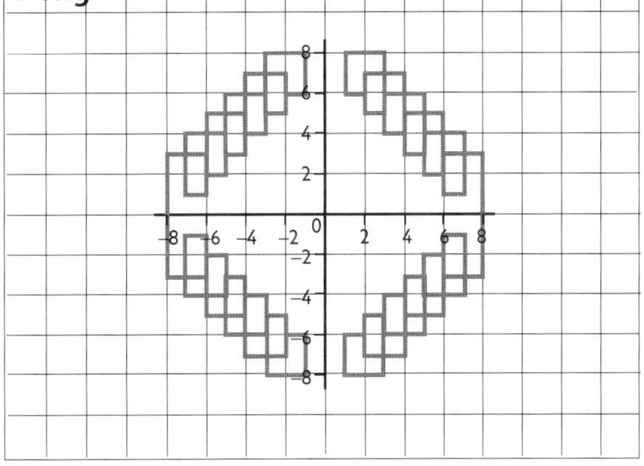

33 The race

We need to calculate how many kilometres each animal travels every day; dividing this into 300 gives the number of days taken.

Finishing dates and times:

Animal	Finishing date	Approximate finishing time
Hare	12th January 2000	10:05
Crocodile	15th January 2000	11:51
Tortoise	24th January 2000	11:30
Ant	14th March 2000	7:53
Snake	9th July 2001	13:40

34 How now? Which cow?

The difficulty here is that not only do we need to compare metric and imperial measures, but that the cows' outputs are quoted over different time periods. One solution is to convert each cow's output to pints per week; these can then be matched to the needs of the different villagers.

The solutions are given to the nearest pint per week, with the suggested destination village given in brackets.

Bell gives 234 pints per week (Nerdowell)
Buoy gives 108 pints per week (Poresdown)
Chpotato gives 308 pints per week (Old Doodle)
Slip gives 169 pints per week (Whapper)

35 Getting classrooms on-line

The children need to think about the problem before they begin to make calculations. They should organize these so that it is easy to see how much of each type of track is being used in their layout.

36 Baby Bighead's building bricks

The impossible numbers are the 24 primes: 17, 19, 23, 29, 31, 37, 41, 43, 47, 53, 59, 61, 67, 71, 73, 79, 83, 89, 97, 101, 103, 107, 109 and 113.

All other numbers can be found as the product of the prime numbers represented on the bricks. Baby Bighead is right, since of the 111 numbers between 10 and 120, he can make 87 from his bricks.